GRATI
TUDE

First Edition
Published in Great Britain by Mindspace Press

Author: Adam Dacey
Copyright Mindspace 2019

Typeset: Sakura Dao
Proofreader: Lyndsay Hill
Cover Design: Tian Du
Copyeditor: Hannah Danson

Printed and bound in Cornwall, England by TJ International
Font used: Garamond

A CIP catalogue record for this book is available from the British Library.
ISBN:978-1-9164838-1-1
First Printing. September 2019

Mindspace Press
Moseley Exchange,
149 Alcester Rd,
Moseley,
Birmingham,
B13 8JP

For more information, online resources, questions, and review, please contact:
info@mindspace.org.uk, 07908950871, www.mindspace.org.uk

Guide to the **Grateful** Way of Life

MINDSPACE PRESS

Adam Dacey

CONTENTS

CHAPTER 3
GRATEFUL BREATHS

Using our breath wisely

CHAPTER 4
GRATEFUL SEEDS

Identifying with our potential

CHAPTER 5
GRATEFUL EATING

A delicious life

CHAPTER 8
GRATEFUL FUTURE
Confidence and positive decisions

Preface

It was the spring of 2019, and the night before a family wedding. I thought about the time, effort and care we take to prepare and plan our outfit when attending such events. This lead to me thinking about how much effort, if any, we spend considering our inner outfit, our state of mind and attitude; the prior preparation that we give to this, and the attention during the day we exercise in maintaining this inner outfit. Do we give this any time at all?

We can ask the same question about our life. How much time do we take to look into the mirror of our mind, preparing it, and making it presentable for the outside world, compared to the time we spend making our outer selves presentable?

As I was considering this, I noted my mind was about to dwell on thoughts of a person at the wedding with whom I have had a long history. I could see that I was thinking about what they hadn't done for me and the gaps in their care and attention. I tried to step back from this stream of slightly negative-tinged consciousness and asked myself the question: 'What about what they *have* done?' There was a little resistance within my mind to consider this. I tried it again. 'What about what they *have* done?'. I followed this way of thinking a little deeper and exercised some focus and concentration; as a result, I managed to open the door to gratitude in my mind.

That evening, when a friend asked me how I was feeling about the day, I said hopeful and grateful; this response then initiated an uplifting conversation.

On the journey to the wedding I mentally renewed my intention to keep a positive, grateful mind. As I arrived at the wedding ceremony, I acted on this intention and decided to make all my interactions positive, by being mindful of the intention I had set and utilising the momentum it had created.

When I saw the person in question, I renewed my intention and encouraged gratitude for what they had done. It worked, and my mind remained calm, happy and peaceful.

Later in the day, when the wedding had progressed through to the reception and dinner, we had the speeches. During one of the slightly longer-than-wished-for dialogues, someone I was close to became visibly upset and needed to leave the room. A short while later, when the speeches had concluded, they came to stand next to me. We were on the edge of the main room surveying the unfolding of the evening's events. I asked if everything was okay. They said, "You know, I was just thinking about what they haven't done," and then proceeded to list several upsetting events from over ten years ago. They were following the train of thought that keeps the door of gratitude closed. We had been over this subject together many times before. I listened. I could have stoked the points raised and opened a negative door for both of us. When they had finished, I said, "What about if we think what they *have* done?" It was a full stop. The grateful door had been opened. They paused, pivoted, thought and, without any frustration, said, "Yes, we could do that." We had walked through the grateful door; as a result, our subsequent conversation was positive, and so were the further interactions throughout the evening.

As I left the wedding, the grateful mind and decision to keep it were still there; the intention to consider what they had done, not what they hadn't. Not only that but this was a mental catalyst to be able to look around at my life and see what I'd received from others, to see my good fortune and awake to the richness right in front of me.

Gratitude can help us and, if we learn to train our mind, can help all those around us, thus making a difference in our world. Behind the grateful door there is an uplifting, happy, positive, enriched and satisfying world. We can open this door at any moment during our life. We are not denying the challenges or suppressing them. We are choosing where to place our attention and what thoughts to invite into our mind, empowering ourselves with the freedom to be able to let go of ways of viewing the world that lead to stress, unhappiness and disharmony. When we open the grateful door, we don't just walk into a room, we access a new world.

I set an intention, encouraged myself to put this intention into practise, was mindful of the intention and allowed this intention to influence my view; as a result, I witnessed how gratitude can transform a situation.

As you are reading this book, test the practices and see if they work in your daily life. Give yourself time. There is a practice for each day. If you are not in a rush to see instant results, you will surprise yourself. Anything worthwhile takes time. Consider the growth over time of a great oak.

I recounted this story at one of the live classes that I teach. One student said that they were dreading attending an upcoming wedding due to the likelihood of having to meet someone with whom they had a challenging relationship. Reflecting on the above way of grateful thinking, they felt confident that, with a little focus and determination, they would be able to mentally move on, and let go of the stress and negativity arising with respect to this pending interaction.

Another student asked the question, "What about if you can't think of anything to feel grateful for or positive about concerning the person in question. What if they haven't done anything for you?" I answered, "With a creative, positive, proactive mind, there is always a way. For example, you could generate gratitude for the opportunity this relationship is offering you to practise patience (we will explore this theme in Chapter Seven) and, as a result, increase your ability to have one of the most essential, helpful mental skills on the planet." Another student considered the wedding story and asked, "What if you encourage another to be grateful and they can't shake off the negativity?"

The nature of our relationship with someone will determine how we can help them: what we say, what we don't say, how we say it, and the intention behind what we are saying — also having the patience not to expect immediate change.

Appreciating the most effective way to help those around us is to continually change our mind, and show an example of training in the actions of our body, speech and mind.

I feel very fortunate to be able to write this book, while also teaching live classes in the community. This gives me the chance to share the training, deepen my own practise, and see the profound impact that gratitude has on people's lives. Also, to explore questions and doubts around these themes and then to be able to share these with you in this book. I have noticed over the years of teaching that similar questions arise relating to each specific theme. If we can resolve these, we will have clear confidence and energy to practise whole-heartedly and thereby gain deep and profound experience.

There are many levels of gratitude. We must start where we are, be realistic with our training, and not enforce an exaggerated expectation on our growth. With a consistent focus, we can develop and learn to transform any situation into our gratitude practise. Taking our time, step by step, we can grow this precious mind within our heart.

When I was growing up, there used to be a cinema that we visited which only had three screens. As you went down the patterned, slightly musty, red-carpeted, windowless corridor to the two small screens, you could choose to go into screen two or screen three. The choice was yours. In that era, you could choose between films like *Room with a View* or *Top Gun*! It is the same with our life and the direction we are heading in. We can choose which film, which version of our life, we are going to watch at any given time by deciding which mental door we are going to open and enter. This decision will then influence the world that appears to our mind.

This book opens the door of gratitude. What we will realise as we turn the pages is that we have opened this door many times already. It's not a new door, or a unique experience, but what this book and course offers is the method to keep opening the door, exploring the world of gratitude when we go through it. We will explore how we can create a grateful habit that will uplift our mind, restore and stabilise our mental health, bring healing to our relationships, increase the resilience in our heart, and protect us from negative attitudes in the future.

When I first taught this theme in the Buddhist temple, I would title and refer to the gratitude class as, 'The Natural Prozac'. At that time, Prozac was taken to treat depression. Fast forward to today and we can see there are now many more medications available and widely taken for depression, with an increasing number of people being prescribed them. This text doesn't claim to function in the same way as these pharmaceutical medications; however, the practices, if taken personally, will help to uplift our mind, improve our positive mental attitude, and increase our inner strength. In today's busy, distracted world, where mental health issues are on the increase, there is no more important activity that we can engage in for ourselves and the people around us than to train our mind and encourage the growth of gratitude.

The mind of gratitude is the foundation for all positivity. If we can establish it within our consciousness, we can gift ourselves a stable foundation for a happy life. By encouraging this positive mind to grow, we and all those around us will come to enjoy all the incredible, practical benefits that it brings.

Introduction

This book offers a series of gratitude reflections and mindful meditation practices. Through slowly and carefully following the guided practices presented, we will come to enjoy all the benefits of having this uplifted mental attitude within our own experience. Each section encourages a positive motivation to seize every moment of this short, precious life.

The great Tibetan meditator, Geshe Chekhawa, from the twelfth century, was renowned for having a peaceful smile on his face; he proclaimed in his text, *Training the Mind in Seven Points*.

"Always rely upon a happy mind alone."

Wise advice, which, if practised in today's busy, distracted world, will have transformative consequences. Reflect on any circumstance you are currently experiencing and consider: Would this feel, appear, seem different, if filtered through a happy mind?

The happy mind we are referring to in this context is a state of mind influenced by gratitude and emotional intelligence; a mind that is stable, resilient, peaceful, and uplifted. When we are influenced by the mind of gratitude, we can find mental solutions to the issues and challenges that arise in our daily life. We can learn how to transform our inner conversation and uplift our mind in any situation.

What interested me when I first learned this practice was that I could 'train' in the process of developing a grateful mind. Having a happy mind of gratitude didn't depend on the quality of my external situation.

With care, attention, and skill, we can train to nurture and grow the experience of gratitude inside of us. Even without training, gratitude arises naturally within. When someone shows us kindness, we say 'thank you'. We express our gratitude. With practise we can encourage this mind to arise more frequently. We can learn to shine the light of gratitude on our everyday life. The more we can cultivate this skill the richer our experience of each moment will be.

In the same way that we can train the body to become strong, fit and healthy, so can we train our mind. A strong mind comes from having a positive mental attitude, and gratitude is the foundation for all positive attitudes.

This grateful attitude doesn't necessarily need to display itself externally. It is a peaceful, humble, balanced mind that acknowledges the great fortune we experience in our life, and the kindness that we receive from others. It may lead to a self-confidence that we choose to express to the world, or it may empower us to quietly work on behalf of the welfare of others.

Our mind naturally follows habits, and it is easy to drift into auto-pilot where we can take the abundance in our life for granted. Gratitude becomes like our best friend, helping us to wake fully to each moment of good fortune in our life. Developing this mental skill is like acquiring a refresh button which we can press whenever we choose, guiding us to look at our world through a clear, positive lens.

When we train in mindful meditation, the starting point for cultivating positive mental attitudes is encouraging our mind to see the world through the eyes of gratitude and appreciation. Training in gratitude uplifts and directs our mind toward an experience of happiness. Gratitude naturally arises if we can take all the opportunities presented each day to live in the moment and are mindful of each of our experiences.

Through following the instructions and practices contained within these eight chapters, we will learn, step-by-step, how to develop and mindfully cultivate this positive mental attitude, so we can feel empowered in every part of our life. Through reading and engaging with the content, we will eventually be able to cultivate the mind of gratitude in all circumstances, regardless of our external situation.

If we are focused and determined, anything is possible. Bringing an experience of gratitude into the centre of our life will help to enrich our everyday experience, and uplift our mind, while being grounded in the present moment.

Each of the eight chapters within this book presents a new theme with seven separate practices to enjoy each day, over two months.

For the adventurous, follow the book as an eight-week course and experience all the benefits. Alternatively, read in one's own time, pick and mix, while receiving daily inspiration. At the end of each day, there is the suggestion to write down our thoughts and engage with the suggested exercises to empower our further engagement with the content.

An important part of this book is the *Notes and Discussion* section at the end of each practice. This helps us to engage with the content in a more proactive way. Discuss with a friend, discuss online, and/or write some thoughts down in your notebook about the questions asked.

In addition, a helpful practise while working through this book is to write down five gratitudes from the day. This writing exercise is a powerful method that can help us review our day with a positive, uplifted attitude and fall asleep with a peaceful, grateful mind.

Connecting with this reflection at the end of each day allows us to become influenced by positivity, thus affecting the mind that we have when we fall asleep, the states of mind that we have when we are dreaming, and also the quality of the mind we possess when we wake. Try to make the intention while you are reading this text to engage with this exercise. When I first delivered this course over an eight-week period, the participants found this particularly helpful.

I give an example below of five things at the end of the day we could feel grateful for, to provide an insight into the type of content that we could write:

1) I had the time and freedom in my life to be able to spend quality time this morning in peaceful meditation.

2) I was able to enjoy a healthy brunch and have this nourishing food sustain me throughout the day.

3) I had physical health in my body which allowed me to cycle to the train station through a nature reserve and enjoy this beautiful natural habitat.

4) I was able to slow down and notice the small buds of rose flowers that had appeared in my garden.

5) I was able to cast my vote at the election, due to being born and living in a democratic country.

The cornerstone for gaining the most from this book is taking time each day for quiet reflection. Reflection on gratitude helps to identify this precious mind and encourage its growth and development. Through integrating our experience from quiet reflection into our daily life, we become fluent with this positive mental attitude and acquire confidence and power to effect authentic change.

In Chapter One, we explore the process of how to reflect on gratitude and cultivate the strength of mind and intention to carry our experience. The key to making progress while reading this book is to connect each day with the content, mixing our mind with the practices in both a formal and informal manner.

Just a short practice, even for a few minutes, will help us move forward. Making progress with and cultivating gratitude will bring happiness into our mind, regardless of our circumstances.

All we need is around ten to fifteen minutes each day, maybe some days maybe less, some days a little bit more. Over the weeks and months, you will start to gain experience.

The content of this book may be entirely new, or we may have some experience; either way, try to approach the training with a beginner's mind, keeping a fresh, open attitude.

The simple act of gently reading each page will support you in feeling uplifted and hopeful with life, and confident with who you are in this ever-changing world.

When you see this sign, ❖, it is an indication for you to take your time, read, reflect slowly, and meditate. A further ❖, marks the end of the meditation section.

Grateful Meditations

Starting with peace

Day 1

Schedule: Creating our gratitude plan

It will be helpful to decide on a practice schedule when you are reading and engaging with this book. Reflect on what you wish to accomplish by the time you have completed the book. The experience you gain will hinge on the amount of time that you put aside to practise.

How much time each week do you currently feel that you can give to your gratitude practise?

a. Just a weekly experience, a little trickle of happiness coming into my life.
b. Well, you know, I am interested and prepared to do a few sessions each week.
c. Maybe every other day, one day on, one day off.
d. I'm going to try and practise each day.
e. Like a Zen monk, I'm going to be doing this every day without fail!

So, have a little think and make a plan. If you wish, sit down and quietly reflect on your schedule. Mentally design your next eight weeks. Even write down in a notebook what you hope to accomplish. Try as you progress through the book to revisit your initial plan; renew, refresh, and update.

You can use the above a) to e) letters if you wish, or write a note to yourself. If it helps, make a reminder on your phone or chat with a friend and share what you want to accomplish. Even make a public post on social media, for example:

Dear friends, today I am starting a book called, Guide to the Grateful Way of Life. I will be training in gratitude each day to bring happiness into my life, and I hope to share this with you.

Once you have finished the book, make a note of how you wish to continue, and then from time to time revisit this.

That's it for today. This relaxed, but focused planning, will gently guide you over the course of these eight weeks into a grateful way of life.

Engage in discussion with a friend, and/or write some thoughts down in your notebook.

Notes and Discussion

How much time would you like to give to your gratitude practice?

How important do you think it is to make a gratitude plan?

Write down several reasons you can feel grateful right now?

At the end of your day, write down five gratitudes.

Day 2

Motive: Setting our intention

We set our motivation for the time and effort that we will put into our training over the next two months. Our mental health, inner development, and happiness will increase each day if we reflect on gratitude. Also, if we are sincere in our training, our friends, family, and society will benefit greatly.

The most positive intention that we can set for our training is:

I am going to train in gratitude meditation over these next eight weeks to bring peace and calm into my life, and then to share my experience with all those around me. Over time, my gratitude practice will benefit my friends, family, community, all those in my society, and finally everyone from across the world.

This intention brings compassion into our practice, which means our practice will have significant meaning in not only helping us but also all the people in our life. So, let us set this motivation, ideally spend around ten minutes on the reflection set out below, or just gently read it (make it longer or shorter depending on your schedule).

Sit in a relaxed, upright posture. Gather your attention into your body.

Become aware of your surroundings; dissolve your distractions into the present moment. Allow your body and mind to settle.

Bring your attention to the sensation of the breath and count the out-breath, see if you can count ten rounds of breathing. If your mind becomes distracted, come to the first round again.

After a while of engaging in mindful breathing, quietly set this intention:

I am going to train my mind in gratitude to bring peace and calm into my life and then to share my experience with all those around me, so my practice will eventually bring benefit to my friends, family and finally, the whole of society.

Try to reflect on this intention for a few minutes.

When it arises strongly in your mind, hold it single-pointedly for as long as possible.

When your mind becomes distracted, return to the reflection until the intention arises clearly. Hold this intention gently in your mind.

Make the intention to carry your experience into your daily life, so your intention will grow, naturally and organically.

...

We try to keep this motivation whenever we read the book and train in the practices. This intention will bring power to our training and inspire us to continue practising and to remain focused, understanding that our practice will have positive effects on all those around us.

Engage in discussion with a friend, and/or write some thoughts down in your notebook.

Notes and Discussion

How important is your motivation in this gratitude training?

Do you want to include your friends & family in your motivation?

Write down several reasons you can feel grateful right now?

At the end of your day, write down five reasons to be grateful.

Day 3

Settle: Learning how to calm the mind

For us to gain a deep experience of gratitude, it is important to develop the ability to settle our mind so we can be less distracted by wandering thoughts. The way to accomplish a settled mind is by spending time with the following practice.

We learn to allow our thoughts into our mind and not fight or suppress them; letting them flow past like clouds moving gently across the vast blue sky of our mind.

Ideally, engage with this training for around ten minutes. As time passes, try to gradually increase the length of time that you practise. Initially read the text slowly, over time start to memorise so the practice can be engaged in with our eyes closed. It is also possible to practise using the audio recording, which you can access when you enrol on the gratitude course.

Tailor the following session to your schedule. You could read slowly, spend a few minutes reflecting. Maybe take ten minutes out of your day to quieten your mind and gain insight, or spend even longer, depending on your wish and intention.

Sit in a relaxed upright posture, gently and gradually bring your attention into your body.

Start to become aware of your surroundings.

Notice the movement in your body.

Let yourself relax.

Let your body and mind settle. Gently close your eyes.

Bring your attention to the sensation of your breath, notice the complete in-breath, and then the out-breath.

As you breathe in, allow your back to straighten and your chest to open.

As you breathe out, let your shoulders drop and relax.

As time passes, start to count the out-breath.

See if you can count ten rounds of breathing.

If your mind becomes distracted, return to the first round.

Bring your wandering mind to the sensation of your breath.

When your mind gathers, turn your focus inward.

Start to notice the activity within your mind.

Observe with a non-judgmental attitude, try not to stop your thoughts, watch your mind and observe.

Reflect that your thoughts are like clouds passing through the sky of your mind. They arise and dissolve, just like clouds.

If you are patient with this reflection, over time it can be beneficial for settling your mind.

Spend a short time just sitting and watching, inviting thoughts, but not entertaining them.

Try not to expect instant and immediate results and be patient enough with yourself to allow your cloud-like thoughts to dissolve.

As your session concludes, recall your compassionate intention from yesterday and determine to be mindful through your day.

...

Notes and Discussion

Feeling creative? Why not draw what a settled mind feels like?

How can you begin to bring pockets of calm into your day?

At the end of your day, write down five reasons to be grateful.

Day 4

Natural: How to cultivate gratitude

When we start our gratitude training, it is important to have confidence that this is a state of mind we already possess, it is not a training that we need to start from scratch. With skilful reflection, we can tap into the gratitude already within our mind.

When we train in gratitude, we are not creating and connecting with a new or fabricated experience. We already have the mind of gratitude. Appreciation arises naturally throughout the day. Check, when somebody shows us kindness, we say 'thank you'.

Sometimes we wish to show our appreciation by sending a card or a present to express our gratitude. This expression is a warm, friendly and open feeling. Today, in this contemplation, we are going to reflect on these moments of gratitude that we have had in our life thus far and bring them to mind.

This practice is to help give us confidence that the gratitude we are exploring in this text is something already in our possession.

When we train in the mind of gratitude through this book, it is helpful to establish the mind afresh, not just to rely on previous experiences. This is so our experience is not just intellectual, but is alive, and functions to bring happiness into our life. However, here in the early stages of our training, we are taking the time to appreciate the gratitude inside us that we have generated in the past.

Please bring your attention to your body while sitting in a relaxed, upright posture.

Gently become aware of your surroundings. Allow your body and mind to settle into the present moment.

Bring your attention to the sensation of your breath and begin to count the out-breath, count ten exhalations, several times.

When your mind wanders, gently return it to the sensation of your breath.

Reflect on a time in your life when someone has shown you kindness and helped you in some way.

Go back to this time; try not to just remember what happened when you had the experience but what you felt when you received the kindness; how was that feeling?

Maybe you still have this feeling of gratitude towards the person.

Try to revisit this mind and bring it to the forefront of your consciousness.

When this mind of gratitude arises clearly, try to hold it with your concentration for as long as possible.

If the mind fades, return to your contemplation to bring it to mind.

If you become completely distracted, use the sensation of your breathing to refocus your mind, and start the contemplation again.

Continue in this way for the duration of your practice.

When you decide to bring the session to a conclusion, determine to carry gratitude into the rest of your day.

Also, try to remember your motivation that you set at the beginning of the book and dedicate all the positive energy from your practice so that many people in your life will benefit from your gratitude reflection.

...

When we finish our reflection, and it is time to interact with others, we try to remember the kindness that they show, and have shown us, and bring this to mind. We allow the attitude of gratitude to influence us throughout the day.

Notes and Discussion

Write down the experiences and people you are grateful for in your life.

How important is gratitude if you wish to have a happy life?

Write down several reasons you can feel grateful right now?

At the end of your day, write down five gratitudes.

Day 5

Reflection: Stabilising with gratitude

When we train in the gratitude practice, we engage in reflection and concentration. Today we are going to gain experience of reflection and, tomorrow, concentration.

This entire book is a reflection on gratitude. Each week we will explore different ways to bring this precious mind into our life. Today is our opportunity to learn how to engage with this reflection by taking time to appreciate our life, with all the possibility that it affords.

Engage in the below practice for around ten minutes; or make it longer or shorter depending on your schedule. Gently read, and take your time.

Please bring your attention to your body and sit in a relaxed, upright posture.

Become aware of your surroundings.

Start to notice the sounds around you.

Allow your body and mind to settle into the present moment.

Bring your attention to your breath. Notice its sensation as it enters and leaves your body.

If your mind distracts, notice the wandering.

Watch your thoughts like clouds passing through the sky.

After a short time, when your mind settles, engage in the following gratitude reflection. Consider the positives in your life right now; keep it simple, even just taking one thing to use to generate this mind.

I am alive. Follow your breath gently. *Begin to appreciate the good fortune you have in possessing a human life. Reflect on all the freedom and opportunity that it provides. Consider how lucky and fortunate you are.*

Engage in the reflection in a focused, relaxed way.

When your mind loses its focus or becomes distracted, bring your attention to the breath, stay with your breathing until your mind has settled, and then return to your contemplation.

Continue in this way for the duration of the reflection. Allowing the mind of gratitude to arise, having reflected on your good fortune in being alive.

To help you stay focused, engage in the following mindspace motivation:

Breathing in, I generate gratitude for being alive.

Breathing out, I let go of stress and tension in my body and mind.

When you are ready to bring your session to a conclusion, determine to carry the mind of gratitude into the rest of your day and night.

Also, remember your compassionate intention that you set at the beginning of the book and dedicate all the positive energy from your practice so that many people in your life will benefit from your gratitude reflection.

...

Something extraordinary happens to us when we reflect on gratitude. A gentle smile appears on our face. Whenever I write about this subject or deliver a class on gratitude, I can feel the healing effect that it has on my body and mind. Allow this to happen for you as you are reading the book. If you take your time, your mind will relax, and your face will loosen, that encourages a calm smile to appear. I like to call this 'The Buddha Smile'. A warm, happy, and peaceful experience. When you then look up from the book and out at your world, there will be a softness in your eyes and an openness in your heart; this will naturally uplift your mind and allow you to transcend the stress of modern life.

Notes and Discussion

Do you think focusing on your breath can help you to generate gratitude?

Write down several things you feel grateful for right now.

At the end of your day, write down five gratitudes.

Day 6

Calm-Abiding: Training in mental peace

Yesterday we engaged in a gratitude reflection. There are many ways to approach this contemplation, which we will explore throughout this book. The function of all these reflections and meditations is to encourage gratitude to arise in our mind. Today we are going to start to train in calm-abiding to help stabilise these reflections.

Learning to calmly-abide helps to deepen our understanding and leaves a long-lasting impression on our mind. We cultivate inner strength and stability of mind, which results in being able to carry our reflections into daily life. We are going to use the reflection that we introduced on day three, where we consider a time in our life when we were grateful. Bring this time to mind and allow the precious mind of gratitude to arise. At the beginning of our training, this is a very effective way to connect with an authentic experience. It is encouraging to remember that gratitude is a state of mind that we already have, and these practices function to encourage and nourish its growth.

When we train in calm-abiding using gratitude as our object, we use the power of mindfulness in our contemplation to notice when our mind becomes distracted. We try to immediately bring our mind back and away from distraction to focus on gratitude. If our mind becomes completely distracted, wherein we start thinking about something else, we return to our contemplation to try and stimulate the experience of gratitude once again.

Calm-abiding means that we try to hold gratitude gently in our mind from moment to moment, in a calm, relaxed way. If we can accomplish this, we will be in a position where it is as though we become the mind of gratitude. In the Buddhist meditation texts, they state it is like water mixing with water. As though we, and the mind of gratitude, become one. It is not as though we are looking at the mind of gratitude or in any way separate from it. If we can train in this way it will mean that, in meditation, we become the mind of gratitude.

You can see how this happens, for example, with the emotion of anger. If our mind is angry and we are completely influenced by it, it's as though we become the mind. It takes over our physical, emotional and mental state, and we and those around us have to suffer all the harmful consequences of having its presence within our mind.

If we can become one with the mind of gratitude, it can bring great positivity into our mind, improve health in our body and have a healing effect on all those we encounter.

When we train in calm-abiding initially, we may only be able to hold this mind for a short period, perhaps one or two seconds. As time passes and we keep practising we can progress to five seconds, and then ten. If we keep training, we can grow our capacity to focus up to one minute, and then five minutes, and gradually to one hour. We have the potential to focus single-pointedly on the mind of gratitude, eventually with a trained mind, for as long as we wish, all day if we like!

In just the same way, we can see how there are human beings on the planet who have trained their bodies so that they can complete ultramarathons. To do so they have been focused on their training and built up their physical capacity. They had to start somewhere with their training, even if at one point it was just a short walk. So with our mental training in gratitude, we make a start. With a focused mind, clear intention, positive motivation, creative imagination, and confidence in our potential, anything is possible. Let us now try this calm-abiding training.

Sitting in a relaxed, upright posture, please bring your attention to your body.

Become aware of your surroundings. Try to connect with where you are through your senses.

Listen to the sounds around you.

Experience the sensation of the floor or chair that you are sitting on against your body.

Notice the activity of your mind. Let your mind roam free, try not to immediately restrict it.

Allow your mind to come into your body and naturally settle into the present moment.

Bring your attention to the sensation of your breath. Follow its natural flow. Begin to count the out-breath; see if you can count ten rounds.

Whenever your mind wanders, calmly bring it to the sensation of the breath.

After a short time, when your mind settles, engage in the following gratitude contemplation.

Reflect on a time in your life when someone has shown you kindness and helped you in some way. Return to this experience. Try not to just remember what happened, but what you felt when you received the kindness. How was that feeling inside?

Bring this feeling of gratitude to mind.

Allow gratitude to arise clearly.

When the mind of gratitude has arisen, try to abide with it from moment to moment, calmly.

If the experience of gratitude begins to fade, immediately return to the reflection to bring it back to your mind.

Once again, mix your attention with gratitude, so that you become one with the emotion; there is no separation between your mind and gratitude.

If your mind becomes slightly distracted, return it to the experience.

Continue like this for the duration of your practice.

As you calmly abide with your mind of gratitude, it is like you are gently holding its hand, not too tight, not too loose. Hold it too tight and you squash it and push it away, hold it too loose and it slips from your mind.

See how long you are able to hold the mind of gratitude.

When your mind becomes distracted immediately bring your attention back to your object of meditation.

When you are ready to bring the session to a conclusion, determine to carry gratitude into the rest of your day.

Try to remember your compassionate motivation and dedicate all the positive energy from your practice, so that many people in your life can benefit.

...

Calm-abiding practice is a mental skill that we can develop gradually through the duration of this text. In the same way that if we train our body regularly, it becomes stronger, so if we train in calm-abiding frequently over time, we will see the resilience and strength in our mind evolving.

Possessing it will help to focus our mind so that we can begin to have an authentic experience of this positive state. With a mind trained in calm-abiding, gratitude will move from being a stimulating intellectual idea and state of mind that we sometimes have, into a transformative emotional experience that we can draw from throughout the day and night.

Notes and Discussion

How long can you currently calmly-abide for?

How long do you think you will be able to calmly-abide by the end of the course?

Why do you think in general our collective attention spans are becoming weaker?

Do you think it is possible in today's world to be able to calmly-abide ?

At the end of your day, write down five gratitudes.

Day 7

Obstacle: Overcoming challenges

We will explore this theme in more depth in Chapter Seven; for today, we explore what we feel are our own challenges to making progress with the mind of gratitude during this book.

It would be wonderful to continually have gratitude in our mind. We would feel uplifted and happy all the time, our relationships would be positive, and we would always feel motivated to make the most of the time that we have as a human, alive in this world. Even though we may wish to generate the mind of gratitude, there are obstacles to developing this mind and today we are going to reflect on these.

Once we gain insight into the obstacles we have for developing gratitude, we can reduce them. The first step is identification. Without reading ahead, what would you say are the main obstacles for you in developing the mind of gratitude? Pause briefly here, close the book and reflect what these may be.

Are they coming from the inside, or outside, or a combination of the two? Spend a few minutes thinking about it, if you have a pen at hand, write down your thoughts.

Here are some of the obstacles that we can face when training in the mind of gratitude:

Distractions. Not putting the time aside to read and meditate on the instructions.

Busyness. Being too busy through the day, so we don't allow ourselves to stop and reflect on the world around us.

A strong egocentric view. Feeling that we have little to be grateful for and others are not that kind.

Boredom. After a few days of focus, our mind can become bored, get distracted and wander off to another activity.

Screentime. Due to spending many distracted hours on the Internet, we don't give ourselves the opportunity for any mind-space to arise, which is vital for the the growth of gratitude.

Quietly reflect on the following instructions.

Please bring your attention to your body.

Allow your mind to settle into the present moment.

Bring your attention to the sensation of the natural breath, notice the inhalation and exhalation for a short time.

If your mind wanders, gently return it to the sensation of the breath.

Turn your attention to the mind, reflect on what is obstructing the development and flow of gratitude during your daily life.

Spend a short time reflecting on this.

Please recognise that you are not these obstacles; they are like clouds passing through the sky of your unobstructed mind.

Consider how you can reduce the power of these obstacles and what steps you need to take.

As your reflection progresses, try to focus on a natural conclusion from your contemplations, that you can apply in your daily life to make progress with this gratitude training.

When you decide to bring the reflection to a close, determine to keep a watchful eye for the obstacles in your mind that prevent gratitude from arising. Please get to know these obstacles, so you can start to reduce and overcome their power.

...

Notes and Discussion

Write down your concluding thoughts from the first week and what motivation you have for week two.

At the end of your day, write down five gratitudes.

...

In this first chapter we have introduced the practice of gratitude and how to begin our reflections. Building on the gratitude that is already naturally within us, we can learn to develop an authentic and nourishing experience. We conclude by training in calm-abiding, and appreciating the potential obstacles that may arise for us during this training. Please briefly read the first section from Chapter Two, as there is a practice that we can do tonight before falling asleep.

Grateful-to-Go

Uplifting the mind

Day 8

Waking: Learning to rise with a smile

When we wake up, one of the very first emotions that we can develop is a disappointment, simply wishing to fall back to sleep! It can take us a while to mentally rise, during which time we can be operating in full auto-pilot mode. Grateful waking allows us to rise with a positive mind and greet our day with joy. We start to initiate the habit of waking up smiling.

Before you fall asleep, determine to rise early with the mind of gratitude. Try to motivate yourself to engage with the reflection below as soon as you rise. As you open your eyes, immediately draw your attention to the breathing. Notice your breath as it enters and leaves your body.

Reflection:

How incredible that I have breath flowing through my human body and have this extraordinary human life! I now have a day ahead of me with so many opportunities.

As you are lying down, reflect on the mind of gratitude. Try to bring gratitude to mind and hold it for a few minutes. If you wish you can then sit up in bed and briefly reflect:

I am not going to waste a single moment of this day; I am going to use it wisely and remember to develop the mind of gratitude, not attitude, for all the experiences that I have.

Set this positive intention for your day.

...

Notes and Discussion

How do you think you could wake in the morning with gratitude?

How important is the first ten minutes of your day?

Do you think you can decide what kind of day you are going to have?

At the end of your day, write down five gratitudes.

Day 9

Water: Quenching our thirst with gratitude

Ideally, we try to engage with this practice as soon as we rise. We can connect with the quiet contemplation and then try to integrate the feeling of gratitude that we generate into our daily life.

Upon rising, when you first encounter water, try to reflect on the following contemplation.

How fortunate I am to have access to water. This water is clean and nourishing, and I can use it for quenching my thirst. Many people worked hard so I can now enjoy this water. All I need to do is turn the tap on, and there it is!

Reflect gently and develop the mind of gratitude.

If you wish to further your contemplation, consider how some people right now in this world don't have access to a water source. They must walk for hours each day to find water, and when they do the only water that they can access is dirty.

Others have access to water but it is not clean or nourishing, and it can potentially endanger their life.

Many people right now in the world are experiencing thirst.

Reflecting on this contemplation, allow compassion to develop for those who don't have access to water.

Focus on the minds of gratitude and compassion for as long as possible.

If your mind becomes distracted, notice this and immediately return to the contemplation. If you start to think about something else, use your breath to settle your mind and resume the reflection.

When you decide to bring your contemplation to a close, make the intention that you are going to remember gratitude the next time you encounter water.

Once you gain familiarity with this reflection, it will mean that every time you interact with water, there is a reminder to develop gratitude.

Dedicate all the good energy from the practice so that you can integrate the experience into your daily life.

...

Following this contemplation, the next time that you turn on the tap, take a drink of water, have a shower or brush your teeth, see if you can shine the light of gratitude onto the activity.

To gain an authentic insight into this, when you first start it is helpful to move slowly, be mindful, so you have the time to catch up with your thoughts

It is important to remember with the training that when you engage in gratitude reflections, be patient and allow the mind to arise naturally. You don't need to force or push the attitude, or simply repeat the words. If you are gentle, mindful and can engage with each moment, gratitude will arise naturally without effort.

Mindfulness and gratitude are inextricably linked. With a mindful awareness of our actions, a natural appreciation of our good fortune arises, which thereby induces the virtuous mind of gratitude within our heart.

Notes and Discussion

How precious is water for you?

How can you remember gratitude when you are using water?

When is it possible to integrate gratitude into your day?

How do you think your gratitude for water could manifest into an external action to help others?

At the end of your day, write down five reasons to generate gratitude.

Day 10

House: Shelter from the storm

Today we are taking the opportunity to develop gratitude for our shelter. If possible, try to engage with this reflection at the beginning of the day. Why is it so helpful to practise at the beginning of the day? If we start the day with a reflection on gratitude, it provides us with a beautiful lens through which we filter our life. We will come to discover how our world is a creation of our thoughts and attitudes. If we flavour our thoughts with gratitude, the world will appear differently to our mind.

As you rise (or at any other time of day), immediately look around your room, and gaze at the ceiling. Yes, you have shelter, which has kept you warm and secure through the night so that you can have a peaceful and restful night's sleep.

Reflect on your good fortune to have shelter:

How fortunate I am to have this shelter and protection. Many people don't have such luxury. Also many animals have to live in the wild without any sense of safety. Yes, it is true, I have 'a roof over my head'.

Try to cultivate the experience of gratitude within, gently.

Allow your mind to mix with this experience of gratefulness, so that you become this mind.

Try to calmly-abide with the mind of gratitude. If you becomes distracted, immediately return it to gratitude. If your mind wanders, use your breath to guide your attention into the present moment.

Calmly-abide.

As your meditation comes to an end, determine to carry your experience into the rest of the day. Also, dedicate the energy from your practice so that all the people in your life can benefit and enjoy a happy mind as a result of your gratitude training.

...

At the beginning of today's reflection, there was encouragement to engage with this practice at the start of the day. If we can practise at the start of our day, we give ourselves a great advantage to be able to carry the mind throughout the day. Morning practise allows us to set the tone for the day, meaning whatever happens to us we have an intention and a positive mental attitude that we can use to keep us mentally on track. Concerning reflecting on our good fortune for having shelter, we can remind ourselves of this throughout the day, whenever we are indoors and protected from the elements. We can also use this gratitude reflection at the end of our day as we are falling asleep in our bed. We are allowing our mind to become reacquainted with this positive mindset before sleep.

Training in gratitude also encourages us to look outside ourselves and consider the plight of others. When we appreciate what we have, we may be more aware of those who currently don't have shelter and cultivate compassion for them. Right now, as we are reflecting on these words, people are living without any shelter from the elements, people are being evicted from their homes, there are people unsure of where they will sleep this very evening. We develop the wish that they can find shelter and protection in their lives. We also determine not to forget our good fortune and to make the most of each moment of our life.

Notes and Discussion

Do you think the more we are grateful for our housing the more likely we are to help those who don't have shelter in their life?

How is your experience of the book and practices thus far, are you able to make the time to engage with the content?

Can you ever have too much gratitude?

When your day comes to a close, write down five gratitudes.

Day 11

Transport: Moving with gratitude

Every day we rely on transport systems and networks to move us through our life. Whether we take public transport, travel by car, cycle or walk, we depend on the hard work and dedication of millions of people who have constructed and continue to maintain the network for us to now enjoy. Like with all these gratitude meditations if we are busy, rushed and stressed when we travel, we can completely miss this.

For us to gain an authentic experience at the outset of our grateful transport training, we need to slow down our actions. This change of pace will give us the mindspace to have insight; without this, all the kindness of others and our ability to develop gratitude for them, will pass us by quicker than a bullet train crossing Japan at two-hundred miles an hour!

The way that we travel becomes habitual. For example, if we take the train to work, we can get used to checking our phone while we wait and then, as we are travelling, distracting ourselves from the monotony once again by scrolling on our phone or reading a book. Sometimes it can be helpful when we are travelling to put our distractions away, allow our mind to come into the present moment and gently reflect upon our good fortune. We can consider the train driver, inspector, all those who are involved in working on the train lines to make them function and remain safe. Also, if we wish to take our reflection deeper, we can consider all those who were initially involved in the construction of the train line and over the years all those who have maintained them in an active state.

A gentleman came to my class who had just retired. He shared with me that his work was on the train lines making sure that they were always functioning, and he would have to travel around at night working on the tracks. It brought to mind that throughout all the train journeys that I have taken, I have never considered this work that takes place.

I have an old school friend who is a train driver, and he works on a particular route six days a week. I use this route once a week; however, he drives the train continually and, as a result of this, I can take this train whenever I like.

The same can be said now as you are reading these words. All the transport systems are in place for us to be able to travel wherever we wish at any time. As we are travelling, if we are too caught up with our own lives, we can miss all this and the endless opportunities that are presented to us to be able to generate gratitude.

If we can generate gratitude when we are travelling this will encourage us to keep a happy mind, which means that when we arrive at our destination we will have a positive outlook.

If we don't consciously train our mind in gratitude, it is easy for us to slip into habituated ways of thinking, only becoming aware of the service that we receive when something goes wrong. Gratitude empowers us to see what is right and develop a continuous stream of appreciation in our mind, thereby producing an inner happiness both for us and the people in our lives.

Sitting in a relaxed upright posture, bring your attention gently into your body

Allow your mind to settle into the present moment.

Gather your attention and start to follow the sensation of your breath.

Watch the current activity within your mind, neither trying to stop or change it. Let it come and go.

As you breathe in allow your mind to become calm. As you breathe out, let go of any stress or worry that has gathered within your body and mind.

If your mind wanders gently return it to the sensation of your breath.

After a short time, when your mind settles, engage in the following gratitude contemplation.

When I travel, I use the cars, roads, trains and buses created through the hard work and dedication of others. Without this work I would not have the opportunity to travel anywhere, and my mobility would be very restricted. Even a short walk requires a smooth pavement or path.

Throughout my life, I have used many modes of transport; all of them provided, created and maintained by others. How fortunate I have been thus far, and how fortunate I will be in the future to be able to continue to use them.

Gently reflecting in this way, cultivate the experience of gratitude in your heart, and try to calmly-abide with it.

Try to mix your mind with this gratitude.

When your mind wanders, immediately return it to gratitude.

If your mind becomes completely distracted, use your breath to guide your attention into the present moment.

When you are ready to bring your reflection to a close, determine to carry gratitude into the rest of your day.

Dedicate the good energy from your practice so that all the people in your life can benefit and enjoy a happy mind.

...

When we arise from meditation and go into our day, we try to remember the experience of gratitude. Especially when we are travelling, remember the kindness that many people have shown through their hard work and dedication. Sometimes we can also see people building and improving the roads; this can seem an interference and an annoyance, forcing us to wait and delaying the fulfilment of our wishes. We can completely transform this mental agitation into a reflection on gratitude, thus bringing patience, peace and calm into our experience.

There is one form of reflection when we sit quietly, read and contemplate; however, what makes our practice more powerful is when we can transform our entire life into a meditation, through remembering the experience from our reflections and integrating these into our day.

All that this requires from us is to make a few simple adjustments in our mind; there is no need to alter anything outside of us, or to make any external demonstration of our practice.

Notes and Discussion

At the end of the day, try to list some of the kindness that you have experienced when you have travelled. Be creative and original with your responses.

Did training in gratitude when you were travelling make any difference to your journey?

Do you think this is a gratitude reflection that you can use regularly?

At the end of your day, write down five gratitudes.

Day 12

Service: Recognising daily kindness

Today is our opportunity to shine the light of gratitude on the service that comes our way. Throughout our life, we are on the receiving end of the kindness of others' service. We can see this clearly when we are in a shop, restaurant or café. With this reflection, we can use the times that we are served to experience gratitude. As we progress, we can also include the times we are on the direct receiving end of others' service, even when we can't see them. It can empower us to gain an authentic experience of grateful service if we can reflect on gratitude at the beginning of the day, and make an intention to practise through the busy times when perhaps our mind is usually distracted.

If we always skip the quiet practices at the beginning of the day, although we will gain some experience, we will always feel as though we are chasing our tail, the busyness of our conceptual thoughts will take over, and we will find ourself running around influenced by stress and anxiety. Once we have engaged in a quiet reflection and meditation, we have much more strength of mind to bring gratitude into our everyday life.

Look out for the services you receive and use each opportunity to generate gratitude.

Being served a cup of coffee.

Someone holding a door open for you.

Seeing someone stack a shelf in the supermarket.

Observing the bus driver taking us to work.

Signing for a delivery in the post.

A receptionist taking our phone-call.

A security guard in a shop.

Being served in the supermarket.

Having our hotel room prepared.

Being able to eat food off a clean plate in a restaurant.

The list is endless; why not make your list today?

We are on the receiving end of an abundance of services from others. We can easily take it for granted, or be so busy we miss it, due to rushing through life; today's reflection will help us to highlight this service and offer our respect.

Sit in a relaxed, alert posture.

Gather your attention into your body.

Allow your body and mind to settle into the present moment.

Bring your attention to the sensation of the breath and enjoy the opportunity to relax into its process, while following its journey around your body.

When your mind wanders, gently return it to the sensation of the breath.

After a short time, when your mind settles, engage in the following gratitude reflection.

Throughout the day, I depend on the service of others. Think about yesterday, reflect on the service that you have received. Reflect on the day that you are about to have and the service that you will be on the receiving end of, to make your day possible.

Reflect like this until an experience of gratitude and appreciation arises in your mind.

When it arises clearly, focus on it and calmly abide.

Moment by moment, try to remain with the mind of gratitude.

When your mind wanders, immediately return it to the experience of gratitude.

If your mind becomes completely distracted, use your breath to guide your attention into the present moment.

As your reflection closes, determine to carry your experience into the rest of the day.

Dedicate the good energy from your practice so that you and all the people in your life can benefit and enjoy having a happy grateful mind.

...

One of the effects of training in gratitude is that it melts the heart and opposes negativity and cynicism. These critical minds function to disturb our inner peace and happiness. When we are moving through our life, if we are not mindful, we can have a neutral mind that takes for granted the services that we use or even a negative mind, that sees faults and criticises the services we experience; this is why complaints departments in service companies are so big!

Here we are deliberately opposing this neutrality and negativity and replacing it with the positive mind of gratitude. The key to success with our training is how we practise. With patience, skill and determination, we can start to have an authentic experience of the inner happiness that arises when gratitude is in our mind.

Of course, other people like to feel appreciated and thanked for their service, so that is one of the benefits of this practice, but we also benefit hugely from having gratitude in our mind. One of the roots of the negativity that arises in our experience is an entitled attitude that opposes the mind of gratitude, which results in being blind to our ability to cultivate appreciation. We can see a world that is not kind, and we feel that we are completely disconnected, thereby creating the foundation for confusion and subsequent unhappy feelings.

Gratitude not only uplifts the mind, but it helps us to feel more connected with others and appreciative of what we have as opposed to what we don't have.

Training in gratitude helps us to make friends with ourself, our life, and the world around us. It is the ultimate positive mental attitude that will bring so many good results into our life.

Notes and Discussion

From today, try to have a brainstorm and write down all the services that you have received from others.

Does having gratitude change the way you interact with others?

Consider five reasons from today why you should cultivate gratitude.

Day 13

Health: Acknowledging our good fortune

Staying alive and being able to enjoy our human life requires physical health. The health in our body is the foundation for all our physical activity. We have had the good fortune to enjoy physical health through our life. Even an action as straightforward as reading these words requires physical health. If we start to train our mind in gratitude, we can gain a deeper appreciation of our health; otherwise, taking our health for granted is the default mode of thinking, the easy option.

Our health can be something that we only appreciate in hindsight and arises when it weakens, and we become sick.

If you currently have some form of physical sickness, please refer to the reflection on day forty-seven in Chapter Seven where you can explore being grateful in adversity; where you can work with, and potentially, transform this challenge.

Today we are going to reflect on our physical health to help us cultivate the mind of gratitude. As with all the reflections in this series, we practise in quiet contemplation, whether that is in our bed, sitting in a chair, sitting cross-legged on the floor, or while we are travelling.

Take ten minutes or so to sit and then look to integrate your experience into daily life.

Gradually bring your attention into your body. Notice the sensation and subtle movements.

Allow your mind to settle within your body, letting go of distractions and thoughts about the future.

Gather your focus and notice the sensation of your breath.

Observe gently how its natural flow and movement affects your physical body.

If your mind wanders or becomes distracted, keep gently returning it to the sensation of your breath.

After a short time, when your mind becomes settled, engage in the following gratitude contemplation.

I have had physical health throughout my life; this has allowed me to accomplish so much. My health has been the basis for all the good experiences that I have had.

Reflect on the breath that is now passing through your body, the blood that flows through your veins.

Regardless of what else is happening in your body, you have some degree of physical health.

Reflect like this until you develop a feeling of appreciation and gratitude.

When this mind arises, calmly-abide with it for as long as possible.

If your mind becomes distracted, immediately recall the reflection, bring gratitude to mind, and hold it again with your focus, trying not to allow your mind to stray.

If you completely lose focus, return to the contemplation again, until gratitude arises, and when it does, release the contemplation and hold gratitude once again within your mind. Try to abide with this mind for as long as possible.

When you are ready to finish your practice, determine to carry gratitude and appreciation into the rest of your day.

This book is designed to ease us gently into the practice of gratitude. As we progress through the stages presented in the text, we can increase our capacity to train our mind and start to confidently address and work with the more challenging elements of our life.

Just as a weight trainer begins with the lighter weights until their strength is sufficient enough to lift heavier weights, which feel very different when the physical body has adapted and shaped, when we train our mind, we start where we are, gently, and gradually increase.

One of the comments that often arises in discussion within my classes is that it can be hard to train the mind. My response is to talk about approaching the training in a way so that it is easy. To do this, we go gently and practise little by little, making steady progress. Not expecting too much from ourselves or being disheartened when we don't observe quick progress. We rejoice in the small developments we make, keeping a happy mind, and feeling grateful.

Notes and Discussion

How can you develop an appreciation for your health?

At the end of your day, write down five gratitudes.

Day 14

Network: Waking up to interdependency

Today is our opportunity to acknowledge the incredible network of kindness that we enjoy each day. If we don't spend time reflecting, it can seem that we are isolated from our community.

In today's world, one of the primary mental health issues is loneliness and a feeling of separation from those around us, especially with the growth of urbanisation, and in many societies, the dissolution of the traditional family structure.

If we reflect quietly and carefully, we will discover that we are not separated or isolated from others. We are completely and utterly dependent on them. Our existence hinges upon being part of an incredible network of interdependency. Our survival depends entirely upon others. In today's reflection, we are going to explore this and carry this awareness into our daily life.

Bring your attention to the location where you are practising. Listen to the sounds around you and engaging with the sensory experience.

Allow your body and mind to settle into the present moment.

Start to bring your attention to the sensation of your breath gently.

Counting your out-breath to help focus your mind, count ten-rounds without distraction.

If your mind wanders, keep gently returning it to the sensation of your breath.

After a short time, when your mind settles, engage in the following gratitude contemplation.

I am part of a complex network that spans the entire planet. My existence depends on all my previous ancestors — every moment of my survival, I depend upon others and their work. To be able to take a simple walk down the street requires being dependent on an elaborate and complex network of millions of people, which goes back centuries consisting of billions of actions of body, speech and mind.

Mentally step back and reflect on this for a short time. Allow your mind of gratitude and appreciation to arise.

When gratitude arises deep within, try to calmly-abide with it, and stay with this from moment to moment, in a relaxed manner.

Mix your attention with the mind of gratitude.

If your mind becomes distracted, immediately recall your object of meditation and hold it again; try not to allow your mind to wander.

When gratitude arises in your mind, try to hold it with single-pointed concentration for as long as possible.

When you are ready to finish your session, make the determination to carry your gratitude and appreciation into the rest of your day.

...

Notes and Discussion

Let's get creative!

Sketch in your notebook your gratitude network from where you are sitting now.

Not keen on sketching? Why not write a short poem about your gratitude network.

Alternatively, leave a blank space and come back when you are ready and the creative juices are flowing. Or, if your creativity flows with music, or dance, or clay, or photography, or fabric, go and use those mediums to explore your gratitude network.

Most importantly, from each session and day of practise, try to carry the feeling of gratitude that you have generated into your daily life.

At the end of your day, write down five gratitudes.

Grateful Breaths

Using our breath wisely

Day 15

Breath: The perfect marriage

I recommend spending around ten minutes on today's mindful training, or simply just read slowly and carefully. Adjust the timing depending on your schedule.

Sit in a comfortable, relaxed, upright posture, gradually gather your awareness into the body.

Patiently let your body and mind settle.

Bring your attention into the present moment.

Let thoughts of the past and future pass through your mind.

If your mind wanders, gently return it to the present moment.

Refocus by using the subtle sensation of your breath.

Feel the coolness at the tip of your nostrils as you breathe in, and the warm sensation as you breathe out.

After a short time, when your mind has settled, engage in the following gratitude practice and contemplation.

While again noticing your breathing, reflect:

I have had the great good fortune to enjoy this human life thus far, with so many opportunities.

My human life is very delicate and precious.

My breath is the very life-force, everything depends on this process.

I currently still have this human life; how lucky and fortunate I am.

As you gently follow the process of your breath, reflect in this way.

Engage in the reflection in a focused, relaxed way, combining it with an awareness of your breathing.

If your mind loses its focus or becomes distracted, bring your attention to the breath, until it is settled, and start combining your gratitude reflection with your breath once again.

Continue like this for the duration of your meditation session, combining your breathing with the reflection on gratitude.

In this way, you are allowing the mind of gratitude to flavour your breathing meditation.

You can strengthen your focus by engaging in the following practice.

Breathing in, I appreciate my good fortune.
Breathing out, I understand my impermanence.

When you are ready to bring your session to a conclusion, determine to carry the gratitude reflection into your day.

Also, dedicate all the positive energy from your practice so that many people in your life will benefit from your gratitude reflection.

...

In our daily life, we use our awareness of the breath to remind us of gratitude. We have so many opportunities to remember gratitude by bringing our awareness to the breathing. This will be our daily practice for the week; when we are not sitting and quietly practising our mindfulness training, we focus on our breathing as often as possible and recall the precious mind of gratitude.

This grateful breath training can be done for short, sharp periods, even just for a few seconds, but most important is that we make a start, to have a gentle practice and try to engage with it as often as we can.

Notes and Discussion

Can you combine gratitude with your breathing during your daily life? How does this influence your mind and activity?

At the end of your day, write down five things that you can have gratitude for.

Day 16

Mantra: Protecting our gratitude training

Mantra is a Sanskrit word which means 'mind protection'. Traditionally mantras are recitations of Sanskrit or Tibetan syllables. In this practice, we are not using these syllables to meditate with, we are going to use our own language to help us to have a more in-depth experience and protect our mind.

We combine reciting unique words of gratitude with our breathing, establishing the mind of gratitude, and then strengthening it by whispering words of gratitude. Later, as our practice progresses, we will mentally repeat these words and, later still, focus on the feeling of these words.

While reciting these words, we calmly abide with our breathing. This mantra training can be useful in assisting us in being able to deepen our focus and ability to mix our attention with the mind of gratitude.

The below practice will be for around ten minutes. You can make it longer or shorter depending on your schedule.

Bring your attention into your body while sitting in a relaxed, upright posture.

Allow your body and mind to settle into the present moment.

As your body becomes still, gather your mind and focus.

Notice the sensation in your body, the contact between your body and the floor, and use this sensation to bring your mind into the present moment.

Start to bring your attention to the sensation of your breath. Count ten exhalations of your out-breath, several times.

Abide with your breathing for a short time.

Briefly cultivate the mind of gratitude, recognising all the good fortune in your life; also reflect on the great kindness that you have received from others. Allow your mind of gratitude to arise.

Now, to help stay focused, repeat the following words to protect your mind from distraction and nourish your grateful mind.

With the mind of gratitude, as you breathe in, whisper the words:

I am so fortunate.

As you breathe out, whisper the words:

Others are so kind.

Whisper these words gently to yourself for several minutes, contemplating their meaning and significance.

To take your practice deeper, mentally repeat the words to yourself, without making any sound:

As you breathe in mentally repeat: *'I am so fortunate.'*

As you breathe out mentally repeat the words: *'Others are so kind.'*

Combine your breathing with the words, mentally reciting and reflecting on the meaning of gratitude.

If your mind becomes hazy or lacks focus, temporarily stop reciting the words and go back to the mindful body and breathing practices to ground you into the present moment.

Engage in this practice for as long as you feel comfortable.

As your session draws to a close, determine to remember your experience within your daily life.

...

The key to making progress with this mindfulness practice is being able to combine the words with the meaning that we have created in our gratitude practice. If we just recite the words without the meaning, they will have little power.

Practising the grateful mantra gives our mind focus and concentration, thereby making it is less likely to become distracted. If our mind does wander, we use the mantra to help strengthen our focus. If our mind completely wanders off, we use our breath to retrain focus, and start reciting the mantra again.

Try at various points through the day to use this mantra and establish a hugely beneficial mental habit of mind. Habits have to start from one single action. If we keep repeating an action, whatever we are doing starts to become a habit.

For example, we have all at some point lived without a mobile phone. We acquired a phone and started to check it. We checked it once, twice, three times, and gradually increased this action. A gentleman at one of my classes recently said that he checked his phone every ten minutes. The habit started at one time with his first check. In the same way we can start creating a habit of reciting the grateful mantra during the day. Even just one time can make a difference and can initiate a grateful habit.

Notes and Discussion

How did you find the use of a mantra influence your focus?

Do you think this is something that you could continue with?

At the end of your day, write down five things that you can have gratitude for.

Day 17

Tree: Exploring our grateful tree

In this gratitude reflection, we use our breath to become aware of the good fortune we possess in having this life. We enrich our gratitude training by contemplating and appreciating our life and its origins.

Firstly, we begin with our parents and we reflect on the kindness that we have received from them in giving us this life. We can go further back and reflect on the kindness we have received from our grandparents, our great-grandparents, and their parents; we keep going back and allow our mind to embrace our family history as far as we can imagine. This is our grateful family tree! Our current existence depends upon an inconceivable amount of kindness received from many generations of our ancestors throughout history.

In some countries they have shrines in honour of their ancestors, where they make offerings and take time to offer remembrance each day. Here we are offering a similar gesture within our meditations and reflection.

In the quiet practice, once again we generate gratitude, this time by contemplating the kindness of our family tree. The mindfulness practice set out below will be for ten minutes. We can make it longer or shorter, depending on our schedule.

At this stage, we don't need to go into too much detail about our family, we are just focusing on their kindness – so that we can allow a mind of gratitude to arise. We will look in more detail at this theme in Chapters Six and Seven.

If you have had a challenging relationship with your family and would prefer not to contemplate this point today, or you have never known your biological family, you could consider another tree of kindness within your network. We will address in detail the more challenging side of the gratitude practices in Chapter Seven, where we explore grateful adversity.

Gently close your eyes and bring your attention to the present moment.

Observe your thoughts as they pass through your mind.

Bring your attention to the sensation of the breathing.

Notice the cool sensation at the tip of your nostrils as you breathe in, and the warm sensation as you breathe out.

When your mind wanders, gently return it to the sensation of your breath.

Briefly cultivate the mind of gratitude, recognising the good fortune that you have had thus far in your life; reflect on the great kindness that you have received from others.

Begin to consider the kindness you have received from your parents in giving you this body that you currently occupy.

Our breath and life depend on this.

Reflect on your entire family tree, try to go further and further back, all the time allowing your contemplation to strengthen the mind of gratitude.

As you reflect further back, allow the appreciation to arise for all those in your family tree, for their existence, their work, and their kindness, understanding that your existence depends entirely on them.

If you see your mind going off point, use your breathing to bring yourself back to the gratitude reflection.

As time passes, pause your reflection and try to focus single pointedly on the mind of gratitude, mixing your attention with it, calmly-abiding with the experience.

When you are ready to conclude your meditation make the determination to carry gratitude through the rest of your day. Dedicate all the positive energy from the training, so you can maintain your gratitude practice.

To help your mind focus, try the following mindful motivation.

Breathing in, gently say to yourself:

Breathing in I generate gratitude for my family.

Breathing out, gently say to yourself:

Breathing out I let go of ingratitude.

If you have the chance to interact with any of your family or see photos of them, take the opportunity to bring to mind this experience of gratitude you have generated in your meditation.

...

Notes and Discussion

How straightforward is it to use your family tree as a method for developing gratitude?

Do you think you will be able to cultivate gratitude when you are next with your family?

How do you think gratitude will affect your family relationships?

At the end of your day, write down five gratitudes.

Day 18

Miracle: Enjoying an essential gratitude practice

Of course, each moment of our life is both precious and rare. We can read books about gratitude, discuss it with our friends, like inspirational posts on social media, even have gratitude posters and reminders on the walls in our house and office, or screen savers on our computer, but how can we internalise this activity so we really can increase our feeling of it within our heart?

The answer: by integrating our practice each day, remaining mindful of holding onto and protecting the precious attitudes we have cultivated, and trying to calmly-abide for as long as possible with the experiences that have arisen from our contemplations. These ways of training the mind are the direct method for internalising our contemplations.

In this practice today, we are going to focus on our breath and become aware of the miracle that we are: of being alive.

The chance and rarity of being born as a human were described by Buddha through using a story. Imagine a turtle that swam around the oceans across the world and floating on this ocean was a large golden ring. Every one hundred years the turtle would come to the surface and stick its head up. The likelihood of being born as the human who we currently are, with the good fortune we possess, is the same as the chance of the turtle coming to the surface of the ocean and putting its head through the ring.

We are a miracle, we are unique, and we are one-of-a-kind. If we can take the time to consider this, it is something that can uplift our mind and open our eyes to the wonder of our existence!

Please bring your attention to the room where you are practising and allow your mind to settle into the present moment.

Start to notice the sensation and flow of your breath.

When your mind wanders from your breathing, gently return it to the sensation of your breath.

Try to sharpen your practice of mindful breathing by focusing on the sensation of the breath as it enters and leaves your nostrils.

Notice the cool sensation as you breathe in, and the warm sensation as you breathe out.

As your attention goes deeper into your breath, reflect how it is sustaining your life.

Reflect on how the life that you currently have has arisen from such improbable circumstances and that the odds for you being alive are almost zero.

Appreciate that you now have such a brief, precious opportunity.

When your mind becomes distracted, use your breath to bring it into focus on your contemplation. As you are breathing, reflect on the miracle of your life. Allow the mind of gratitude to arise.

Continue observing your breath, appreciating the wonder of your existence as you continue with your contemplations.

When your practice ends, make the determination not to waste any moments of your life but to seize it, and appreciate the time that you have left.

...

This grateful attitude means we will seize each and every moment of our precious life. We will not waste our time, clock-watching, killing time, feeling bored, or allowing our mind to become negative. Why? Because we realise the miracle of our life and want to ensure that we don't waste the moments that we have left.

Notes and Discussion

What is so precious about your life?

What moments do you feel grateful for in your day so far?

Is gratitude an emotion that can arise naturally and spontaneously in your mind?

Do you feel like you are a miracle?!

At the end of your day, write down five gratitudes.

Day 19

Gentle: Savouring each moment

When we sample something rare and precious, perhaps a delicious meal or drink from another country and we are told it has unique properties, we may take our time when we consume it, and, if we enjoy it, savour the experience.

In this meditation we are going to acknowledge how rare and fragile our life is, while we are focusing on the breathing. Each time we take a breath we allow ourselves to savour the experience. Seeing our life for what it is, as something quite extraordinary, recognising the humble breath passing through our body and appreciating how it provides us with this precious life.

We connect with the training, allowing our mind to become gentle and positive, fully immersing ourselves with each breath in order to not waste even a single moment.

Bring your attention into the body while sitting in a relaxed upright posture.

Allow yourself to settle and relax in the present moment.

Focus on the sensation of your breath, encouraging your mind to gradually concentrate.

Calmly-abide with your breathing. Each time your mind wanders, gently bring it to the sensation of your breathing.

As you follow your breath, mentally step back.

Allow appreciation to arise for your life.

Consider how it is only due to the breathing that your life is sustained.

Let the mind of gratitude dawn in your consciousness.

When gratitude arises, bring your attention to the breathing and allow yourself to enjoy the complete journey of your breath around the body, taking it in fully, and relishing each breath.

Savour each inhalation and exhalation. With your mind of gratitude, allowing your mind to rest beneath the stress and busyness so you can fully understand the significance and importance of this process.

Continue in this way for the remainder of your session. If your mind wanders and becomes distracted, use the sensation of your breath to return your attention to your practice.

Just before you conclude the session, dedicate all the positive energy from your practice so that you can continue your training in a gentle manner throughout your life.

...

Throughout our day, we try as often as possible to connect with our breath and use this awareness to remind us gently of our precious human existence.

With a creative approach, it is possible to remember this practice many times during our day. For example, when we go to look at our phone, instead of following this desire, we could simply tap our phone, recognise it is there and instead of checking it, we spend time focusing on our breathing while remembering gratitude. After doing this, we could either check our phone or decide not to. In this way, instead of our phone distracting us, it can remind us of our extraordinary positive training in gratitude.

Notes and Discussion

Does your life feel rare and precious? Do you think you can train yourself so that you can encourage this attitude to arise in your consciousness?

At the end of your day, write down five things that you have gratitude for.

Day 20

Drop: The power of encouragement

Without a gentle, careful approach, our mindfulness practice can turn into an activity that we squeeze into our busy lives when we can make the time for it; when we have finished our short practice we return to our 'real life'. It is easy to slip into this habit and will consequently mean our practice always has the feeling that it is separate from our everyday life. With this 'squeeze approach', the beneficial effects of our practice will not trickle through into our existence.

In the grateful training for today, we turn this approach on its head, encouraging ourselves to enjoy and see each moment of our life as our practice. We utilise the precious time that we have on earth as our opportunity to develop gratitude. Our breath is harnessed in this training to help keep our mind focused.

We train in this meditation specifically to decide to develop gratitude in our daily life as often as we can. We try to make the most of each moment and experience of our life.

We can encourage ourself to grow and develop our practice by focusing our attention on our decision making. If we can encourage ourselves at the beginning and the end of the day, we will have the necessary focus and drive to integrate gratitude into our daily actions. When the practice concludes, we immediately try to carry our intention into our daily activities.

...

Gradually bring your attention into the present moment, making the most of the opportunity to stop rushing and pushing.

Allow your body and mind to relax and settle.

As you breathe in, allow your posture to straighten.

As you breathe out, let your shoulders relax and let go of the stress that has built up in your body and mind.

Bring your attention to the sensation of your breathing and begin to count the out-breath, count ten exhalations, several times.

Reflect on the day ahead of you, and the amount of opportunity that you have to generate the mind gratitude.

Allow your mind of gratitude to naturally arise and try to become familiar with it, spend a short time mixing your attention with this attitude.

Gradually begin to make the determination that you are going to carry your experience into daily life. Determine that you are not going to waste a single moment of your day and that you will use each opportunity that you have to cultivate gratitude.

When this decision arises strongly in your mind, try to focus on it single-pointedly.

If your mind becomes distracted, return to your breathing to refocus it, and then return gently to the contemplation and arrive once again at the decision not to waste a single moment of your life.

To help you stay focused as you breathe in with the mind of gratitude, you can whisper to yourself:

I am so fortunate.

As you breathe our you can whisper to yourself:

I am not going to waste this precious life.

As the practice progresses, you can mentally recite these words as you focus on the breath.

When you decide to conclude your practice, make the intention to carry this decision into your daily life.

...

We try to make these practices easy for ourselves, instead of feeling discouraged and thinking how can I possibly practise like this for the rest of my life. Just reflect whether it is possible in the next moment, and the next moment, and the next.

Buddha likened our development to drops of water in a bucket. It doesn't fill up immediately, but over time the bucket fills and overflows. If we patiently focus on staying in the moment, practising moment by moment, keeping it simple, easy, and fun for ourselves, naturally we will make progress with our mindful gratitude training.

Notes and Discussion

Can we make the decision not to waste a single moment?

What would life be like to develop gratitude in every moment?

At the end of your day, write down five gratitudes.

Day 21

Impermanence: Waking up to each moment

One of Buddha's most famous quotes is: 'You should know all phenomena to be impermanent'. In other words, everything is changing. All things are subject to change. They arise and dissolve. When our mind takes a strong mental hold on our world, it appears to stay the same. As a consequence, we can feel stuck in a particular situation or point of time in our life.

The 'grateful impermanence' practise helps us tap into how we change, moment by moment. We tap into our breathing to help us realise this. Due to this awareness, we are naturally uplifted, mentally awakened and motivated to make the most of our changing life.

Bring your attention to the body.

Relax into an upright posture.

Use your breathing to settle into the present moment.

Bring your attention to the sensation of the breath.

Abide with its sensation.

Start to count the out-breath.

See if you can count ten exhalations, several times.

Dwell with your breathing.

Carefully observe the complete sensation of your breath as it enters and leaves your body.

As you are following this process, with one part of your mind recall how you are changing moment by moment.

Reflect:

My body and mind are subject to change; I can't stop this process. Everything around me is changing; as a result of this, I can transform, grow, and experience peace and happiness.

Gently contemplate this as you are following the breathing.

Begin to appreciate each moment as it arises and dissolves.

Start to develop the mind of gratitude for your experience. When this warm, open feeling arises in your mind, hold it with single-pointed concentration for as long as possible.

If your mind loses focus then return it to the sensation of the breathing, regain your focus, continue the contemplation and once again arrive at the experience of gratitude, calmly abiding with this positive mental state. Try to mix your mind with gratitude thoroughly, so you can become one with this attitude.

As your practice comes to an end, determine not to waste a single moment of your life and take the opportunity to 'let go' whenever possible, by remembering your impermanence.

...

Notes and Discussion

How can you embrace impermanence in your life?

How can you stop grasping onto your life?

How can mindfulness practise help you to let go?

At the end of your day, write down five gratitudes.

Grateful Seeds

Identifying with our potential

Along with the rich opportunities that our external world provides for encouraging the cultivation of gratitude, there are also many internal reasons within our mind, which our meditation practice can help us to be mindful of, that will help to enrich and grow our grateful practise.

In the film *Jean de Florette*, a family moves to a farm in France with a dream of the idyllic country life. They encounter great difficulty and hardship in identifying the water source to sustain their farm and crops. Their neighbours know precisely where it is but withhold the information. The family live a poverty-stricken life of misery, spending endless hours and days seeking water, needing to expend tremendous energy travelling to other locations to bring water to their home, even though the source of water is right beneath them. They never discover the water and live out a tragic life riddled with misery.

Similarly, our dissatisfaction can lead us down many physical and mental roads in pursuit of happiness and freedom, while all the time the source of what we are looking for is inside us, within our mind.

Our mind's potential is extraordinary. The stress, agitation and worry that we undergo comes from gross levels of conceptual thoughts. When we can pacify these states of mind through engaging in meditation, we can start to appreciate and enjoy the peace that arises when our mind becomes subtler.

Regardless of our status and position in society, we have incredible potential to experience inner peace and positivity. This chapter provides us with the opportunity to explore this potential and build on our awareness of this by developing the mind of gratitude.

Day 22

Settle: Resting into our essential nature

In this practice we spend valuable time watching our mind, emphasising no resistance. We observe, without attempting to make anything happen. If we are patient, through sitting still and calmly watching our mind, it begins to settle. The distractions of our conceptual thoughts naturally pacify.

We all have the potential to experience inner peace, regardless of who we are, where we are from, and what our status is. Watching the mind and allowing it to settle helps us appreciate this. If we make time to sit still and practise we can begin to discover the incredible peace residing within our mind. The key, as with any development in our life, is making time.

One of the most common reasons I hear for not practising is 'I don't have the time'. It is useful to reflect on this statement and consider whether we are saying 'I don't have the time', or that we are actually saying, 'I don't have a strong enough wish'.

When we have a strong enough intention to do something we naturally make the time. One of the ways in which we can increase our intention to practise is to reflect and consider the great benefits of regular training, both for the person we are now and our future self, and the people in our society and community.

The practice today allows us to gain a glimpse of what it is like to have a settled mind, while we also generate appreciation and gratitude for the chance that we continually have within us to be able to practise. Peace is closer than we think; this meditation helps us appreciate this.

Sitting in a relaxed upright posture, please bring your attention to your body.

Allow your mind to settle into the moment. Observe your thoughts as they pass through your mind; try not to follow them.

Notice the sensation of your in-breath; follow its natural flow. Allow it to gently guide you into the present moment.

Let your mind become one with the process of your breathing.

Turn your attention to your mind.

With an open, non-judgmental approach, observe your mind.

Watch your thoughts as they pass. Let them come and go.

Invite and welcome your thoughts, try not to entertain or spend too much time with them.

If your mind becomes distracted, use your breath as an anchor to the present moment.

Observe your distractions and gradually allow them to settle.

Enjoy this process of watching your mind pacify.

You don't need to make the mind settle; it will settle naturally when the body and mind relax.

As your practice progresses, cultivate a mind of gratitude for the opportunity that you have to experience peace within.

Calmly-abide with the mind of gratitude for as long as you can.

When the time comes to conclude your practice, determine to maintain the awareness you established in meditation through your everyday life.

Notes and Discussion

Why do you think it is that if we sit still and relax, the mind settles?

Is there a way that you can settle your mind each day, how do you think you can accomplish this?

At the end of your day, write down five gratitudes.

Day 23

Calm: Experience calm beneath distraction

Today we take our practice one step further than yesterday's grateful settle training, following a similar style practice where we bring our attention into the present moment and watch the mind. We let our mind settle by just observing it. After a while, we ask the question:

Where is my mind? What is my mind?

We ask the question in an open, relaxed manner as we turn our attention inwards. This question helps us to go deeper into our mind. As we progress to more subtle levels of consciousness we can experience the peace that resides there, beneath distraction and worry.

When we start to enjoy deeper states of mind, we can stop asking the question and abide in the present moment for a short time, quietly observing the mind, letting thoughts pass and remaining in the present moment.

As the practice comes to a close, we take the opportunity to cultivate gratitude for having the opportunity to experience inner peace. This mind of gratitude will encourage us to make the most of each and every moment of our life, inspiring us to train continually in our mindfulness practice.

Please gather your attention into your body and sit calmly, in a relaxed, upright posture.

Allow your body and mind to settle into the present moment.

Focus on the sensation of the breath and try to count each of your out-breaths.

Try to count ten exhalations without distraction. If your mind wanders, note this and start counting from the first round again.

Turn your attention to your mind. Observe your thoughts for a short time.

In the quiet of meditation, ask the open-ended question:

Where is my mind? What is my mind?

Ask this question as you look gently within, gazing inside your mind.

Look beyond and through the busy thoughts.

After a short time has passed, stop asking the question and abide in the present moment. Let yourself go to a subtler level of mind, beyond the distraction of conceptual thought.

Abide in this space for as long as you possibly can.

If your mind becomes completely distracted, use your breath as an anchor to bring your attention into the moment.

As your meditation approaches its concluding stages, cultivate the mind of gratitude and appreciation for this opportunity that you now have as a human being: to train in meditation and experience inner peace.

When you are ready to conclude your practice dedicate the good energy that you have accumulated in your mind so that you can make use of your time and not waste a single minute of your life.

...

It is rare to be born a human being, while also having the inclination to practise mindful meditation (which is the cause of being able to experience inner peace). In this training, we encourage the acknowledgement of this good fortune to dawn in our mind, and allow gratitude to naturally arise.

Through training in gratitude regularly, the motivation organically arises to make the most of each moment and opportunity of our life. Whenever possible, we take the opportunity to train our mind so that we can actualise the potential within us for inner peace.

Notes and Discussion

How you can you ensure that you make the most of every moment of your human life?

Can you feel the existence of calm in your mind?

At the end of your day, write down five gratitudes.

Day 24

Waves: Letting the ocean settle

When training the mind, it can be helpful to have an analogy that we can use, which provides us with an appreciation, connection and insight into the formless world of our mind. As our mind lacks physical form, we can't provide an image of it and say 'this is how the human mind looks'. If I were delivering a live talk on this subject, it would be impossible for me to show during the presentation a picture or photo illustrating to the audience how their thoughts arise and dissolve, and what form and shape they possess.

Today, to help us gain a deeper appreciation of how our mind works, we are going to use an analogy of the ocean and waves. Our subtle, peaceful mind is like a vast ocean. Our busier, conceptual states of mind are like waves that come from the ocean. The distractions that arise continually within us are like waves that disturb the peace of the vast ocean of our mind.

When the waves of distraction pacify through training in meditation, we can start to enjoy the ocean of our mind itself. As a result, progressively, more profound and calm states of mind will naturally arise within, both in and out of our meditation practice.

Remember, this is just an analogy; it is unnecessary to visualise an actual ocean and waves and get mentally caught up in the external detail of the analogy. We reflect on the explanation to help us understand the relationship between our distracting thoughts and our peaceful mind. This description of an ocean to help us understand our mind, has been used for thousands of years to help meditators gain a deeper experience of their mind.

It has worked for many practitioners in the past, and by exploring and enjoying this training, we can follow in their footsteps and come to experience all the great benefits.

Towards the end of our reflection, we cultivate the mind of gratitude for having the opportunity to engage in this powerful training that has been passed down over several thousand years.

After the meditation as we are going about our daily life, we can also explore how the world that appears to us arises from our mind in the same way that waves arise from a vast ocean.

Please bring your attention to the present moment.

Allow your mind to naturally settle, accepting whatever sensations may be arising within your body.

Bring your attention to the experience of the breath; notice how your breath moves through the body. Become aware of your stomach and chest moving as you inhale and exhale. Stay with this process for a short time.

Then turn your attention to the mind.

Reflect how the peaceful mind within you is like a vast, boundless ocean, and your busy thoughts are like waves arising from that ocean.

Your distractions are like the wind that stimulates the ocean of your mind, causing the waves of conceptual thought to arise. The more distractions you have the more waves will arise.

As you are sitting and meditating, you are like a ship sailing on this ocean.

Reflect on this analogy as you are watching your mind.

Gradually stop reflecting on the analogy, and once again observe the mind.

Watch, while remembering and appreciating the understanding that arose from the visualisation.

Permit yourself to enjoy the vast ocean-like mind that lies beneath the distractions, worry, and busyness of conceptual thought.

Abide in this space for as long as you can.

Towards the end of your practice, allow the mind of gratitude and appreciation to arise for the opportunity that you have to experience the ocean of your mind. A precious space beneath the turbulence of distracting thoughts.

...

Once the practice has concluded, we try to keep the reflection alive by applying the same analogy to our everyday life. The appearances that arise moment by moment are like waves which come from the ocean of our root or subtle mind.

We can reflect on how our mind affects the world that we abide in. Notice how, when we wake in the morning with a distracted and agitated mind, the world that appears to this mind is different from the world that we perceive when we wake with a peaceful, calm mind.

We are responsible for the world which we inhabit. If we wish to change the world that we reside in, the most powerful method is to begin to change and alter our mind. The understanding, appreciation and integration of this wisdom into our daily life, helps us develop a deep mind of gratitude for the opportunity that we are currently presented with; to be able to change our world by changing our mind.

No longer do we need to feel helpless and distracted, blaming our experience on others, but instead we can be empowered with gratitude and wisdom to accept responsibility for what we see and take the appropriate steps to change it, by altering our mind.

Notes and Discussion

Do you think that you have the power to change your world, by changing your mind?

What relationship do you feel there is between the world that appears to your mind and your mind?

What do you think comes first – the mind or the objects that appear to your mind?

At the end of your day, write down five gratitudes.

Day 25

Potential: Waking up to the signs

We are building on the training from previous days and recognising the incredible potential within us for inner peace, a state of calm that can completely transform our experience of life. In our world, there is extensive information about the potential that we currently have and steps that we need to take to actualise it. Most of this content focuses on the potential that we have in our worldly life and involves making external changes that will lead to external growth. Many of these methods work and, if we follow them, they can lead to external progress and success.

In today's contemplation, however, we are interested in spending time recognising the potential that we have *within our mind* for inner development, both now and in the future.

In the same way, when gold was first discovered in California specks of it appeared in the river, indicating that close by there was a vast source of this precious metal. If we reflect briefly on the insights already gained from our training of the mind, even if it is just a slight glimmer of the peace that has arisen within our mind, this is an indication that there is more to experience.

Compared to the discovery of gold, the wealth of inner peace is much more significant and meaningful, providing us with the power and energy to solve all of our daily problems and find happiness, regardless of our external circumstances.

The more effort and application we put into learning and training our mind, creating the causes and conditions for inner peace to arise, the more we will gain experience of the calm that is present within, beneath the busyness of distraction.

Everyone has extraordinary potential to experience inner peace. Once we have found the methods for discovering this, it is just a case of applying ourself to the training. We have the seeds to experience a feeling of deep inner peace, contentment and happiness. We have the potential. We have incredible potential. Through appreciating this potential we will naturally apply effort to actualise it, through training in meditation. The practice today is not only a reflection on gratitude; it also functions as a great motivation to make the most of our existence.

Please bring your attention to your body while sitting in a relaxed, upright posture.

Allow your body and mind to gradually settle into the present moment.

Notice the sensation of your breath. As you breathe out, let go of all the distractions, worry and anxiety. As you breathe in, enjoy peace and calm.

Gently turn your attention to the mind.

Look within your mind and begin to recognise the extraordinary potential that you have.

Dwell with this understanding and recognition for a short time.

As time passes, calmly-abiding, allow the mind of gratitude and appreciation to arise. Let this precious attitude manifest within.

When your mind of gratitude arises, calmly-abide with it for as long as possible.

If your mind of gratitude fades, try to renew it by returning to contemplating your great potential.

Once again, when gratitude re-arises try to gently hold it with your concentration.

Alternate like this throughout the session.

You are trying to mix your mind completely with gratitude so that there is no distance between you and this precious state.

When you decide to bring your practice to a conclusion, make the determination to carry the awareness of your potential into daily life.

...

Notes and Discussion

In what ways can you recognise and appreciate your potential?

Do you think that everyone has great potential within their mind?

At the end of your day, write down five gratitudes.

Day 26

Possibility: Appreciating opportunity

We are developing gratitude for the potential within our mind. Within this training we take the time to reflect on the peaceful nature of our mind, spending time just acknowledging this. We then reflect on all the possibilities that lie ahead of us for cultivating our mind and experiencing inner peace.

Many people have the wish to experience inner peace but, due to distractions and other interests, don't make the time to practise. As a result, they are never able to experience the peace and calm that arises from enjoying a settled mind. We now do!

If we have a firm enough intention, we will have plenty of opportunities both now and in the future to enjoy our peaceful mind. Imagine how your practice would evolve if you were to train your mind each day for a year. We allow ourselves in the quiet of meditation to recognise this and develop gratitude for all the opportunities that our life presents.

Please bring your attention into your body while sitting in a relaxed, upright posture, allowing your shoulders to drop and encouraging yourself to focus for the duration of the practice.

Gather your attention into the present moment, patiently letting it settle within your body.

Notice the sensation of your breath and enjoy the opportunity to follow its inhalation and exhalation.

After some time, turn your attention to the mind itself.

Observe your mind for a short time. Allow the recognition to dawn within your mind of the incredible potential that exists within you for the experience of inner peace.

Reflect how, if you were to train your mind, this potential would gradually grow and develop.

You now have the opportunity to experience this.

Also think of all the opportunities that lie ahead of you for being able to train your mind.

Allow your mind to be uplifted by this contemplation — slowly but surely — and allow the mind of gratitude to arise organically within your heart.

As the mind of gratitude arises within your heart, try to focus on it with single-pointed concentration. Stay with this precious mind for as long as you possibly can, calmly-abiding.

If your attention becomes distracted, bring your mind to the present moment through following the sensation of your breathing. When your focus returns, bring gratitude to mind.

When you decide to conclude your practice, make the intention to train your mind, and to seize every opportunity and possibility that presents itself.

...

Notes and Discussion

How can you encourage yourself not to waste the moments of your life?

At the end of your day, write down five gratitudes.

Day 27

Identity: Recognising the positivity within.

Who do we think we are? We all have a sense of identity. We can base this sense of self around our work, our relationships, race, background, our education, our body, the area that we live, the music we like, or the books that we read. Throughout our life, this sense of identity changes.

When we strongly grasp onto our identity we can encounter problems, especially if we take ourself too seriously and meet others who don't. Today we are going to gently start to identify with the deep peace within our mind and try to identify with this peace. As usual, we conclude with the mind of gratitude for being able to recognise the incredible potential within our heart.

We sit and listen to the sounds around us, allowing them to bring our attention to the present moment. Gradually we draw our mind in and away from distractions.

Encourage your mind to stay concentrated through the duration of the meditation.

Observe your thoughts as they pass through your mind.

Watching your mind, allow any distractions and busyness within to pacify, recognising that your thoughts are like clouds in the sky of your mind.

Reflect:

What would it be like if I was to identify with the peace within my mind and to experience the deep tranquillity that arises when one trains continuously in the practise of mindful meditation?

If I thought to myself: 'I am inner peace.'

How would this feel?

Through identifying with the peace within my mind, I can have a more peaceful relationship with myself and find a happiness that arises spontaneously throughout my day.

When there is peace within my mind, I can start to experience happiness and contentment.

We explore this reflection in the quiet of meditation; it is an inner exploration.

To be able to have this identity with peace means you are very fortunate, as you can solve many of the problems which arise from having a negative identity that is caught up with distractions.

To help you focus, engage with the following breathing practise:

As you breathe in, think to yourself:

Breathing in, I am inner peace.

As you breathe out, think to yourself:

Breathing out, I let go of distractions and negativity.

When your mind has refocused return to the reflection.

Towards the end of your inner peace reflection, allow the mind of gratitude and appreciation to arise, for being able to identify with the inner peace in your mind.

Finally, conclude with the determination to stay mindful throughout your life, and to be able to identify with the peace within your mind as often as possible.

...

Our sense of identity can cause us frustration; however, if we train in this meditation, we can enjoy identifying with the peace and potential within. If we try to identify with the peace within our mind, during the break between our mindfulness sessions, we will start to notice the impact that this has on our wellbeing.

Notes and Discussion

Do you think that you can identify with inner peace?

What effect do you think this will have on your wellbeing?

At the end of your day, write down five gratitudes.

Day 28

Gardening: Nourishing the seeds within

The final reflection from the Grateful Seeds chapter is grateful gardening. We have the seeds within us for an experience of great inner peace and contentment. If we water and nurture these seeds, with the right care and attention, growth will take place.

A great oak began somewhere. Consider an acorn: within that acorn there is great potential. Within us, although we can't see directly, there is great potential. In this practice we recognise this, develop gratitude for our potential, and then make the decision not to waste a single moment.

The practice has three parts:

We observe the mind and recognise our potential.

We develop gratitude and appreciation for this.

Finally, we conclude by intending to practise and nourish these seeds.

Consequently, we become an inner gardener as we water the seeds of gratitude within.

Please bring your attention to your body while sitting in a relaxed, upright posture.

Allow your body and mind to settle into the present moment.

Bring your attention to the sensation of your breath and notice its complete journey as it enters and leaves your body.

Turn your attention to the mind.

Allow your thoughts to pass, like waves arising out of the ocean. Relax and step back from the busyness.

Let your mind settle, and allow the recognition to dawn within you of the incredible potential that you have for the experience of inner peace.

Let this reflection bring gratitude into your mind, and try to hold it with your concentration.

Reflect how, if you sow the seeds of inner peace through training in meditation, your experience can become more profound.

Spend a short time positively dwelling on this.

Finally, conclude your reflection to nurture the seeds of peace within your mind, through training in mindfulness and integrating gratitude into your daily life.

Hold this intention for as long as possible with single-pointed concentration.

As your practice comes to an end, determine to carry gratitude in your life and shine it upon all your experiences, while taking every opportunity to watch your mind and enjoy the peace within.

...

Notes and Discussion

How can you remember to water the seeds of inner peace?

Why do you think we are so used to focusing on effects and not causes?

At the end of your day, write down five gratitudes.

This week we have explored Grateful Seeds, identifying and cultivating gratitude for our potential. This gratitude naturally uplifts our mind and motivates us to move forward. When we engage in any mindfulness practice, we are like a gardener sowing seeds. When we sow a seed, we don't expect it to ripen immediately, we are patient and enjoy the process of creating the causes for the ripening.

Recently I planted two cherry blossom trees in my garden. I planted them into the ground as very small trees with no flowers and watered them. It would obviously have been foolish to come back two hours later and wonder why they hadn't grown. Authentic growth takes time. I went to the trees after one week and noticed a little growth. If I nourish and tend the trees, they will grow naturally in their own time, eventually turning into beautiful cherry blossom trees bearing vibrant flowers. Be relaxed in your approach, develop gratitude for your potential and the seeds of peace and happiness will ripen naturally.

So, let's now explore how we can bring gratitude into our life through the practice of grateful eating.

Grateful Eating

A delicious life

This week we are going to explore how we bring gratitude to our eating and drinking. Everyone enjoys these activities; we never forget to engage in them, now is our opportunity during these times to train in gratitude. What is fun about the grateful eating practices is that the training not only helps to progress our mindful training but also enhances our enjoyment!

If we can make a habit of developing gratitude when we eat, we will always have a reminder in our life. Being mindful and having the ability to live in the moment is not difficult; it is just that we easily forget and follow distracting habits. During this week, we have the chance each day to explore how to develop gratitude when we are preparing and enjoying our meals and snacks.

Once this week of practices has finished, there may be one small training from the series presented that resonates. If so, try to use this as a daily practice. On the other hand, you may like to alternate between the practices, experimenting and enjoying the positive effects. If we see our gratitude practise as an organic, holistic process, the training will begin to influence our day, week, month, year and life.

The key to establishing the gratitude habit is consistency. Each day during the week, enjoy a meal or drink and take the time to shine the light of our gratitude onto it. Allow yourself to slow down, be mindful and gently remember the instructions. Ideally, we shine the light of gratitude upon all our experiences; however, sometimes, in the beginning, we may forget, are too busy, or feel overwhelmed with needing to practise all the time.

Taking one time each day means that we can make a start, and the practice will feel light and attainable within our mind. For us to gain experience this week, try to decide each day to engage in the practice and give yourself a little time. It doesn't have to be a long time, just something each day, to keep the momentum of our practise moving forward.

As with all the gratitude training revealed so far, we begin by reflecting skilfully upon the contemplation presented, until we arrive at the experience or feeling of gratitude in our heart. When the grateful feeling arises, we try to calmly-abide with it for as long as possible.

The process of reflection and calm-abiding meditation firstly allows us to gain a correct intellectual understanding to bring about a feeling in our heart, and then through engaging in focused concentration, we try to abide continually with this feeling, so it affects and changes our mind.

One of the indications as to whether the meditations are having an impact on our mind is if we can start to remember the grateful feeling spontaneously during the day, and are able to integrate this beneficial attitude into our life. Gratitude has the power to transform every part of our life if we can apply it to our everyday experience.

Day 29

Shoppers: Awareness of the invisible 'kindness' chain

We start our week with a mindful shop. Today's practice has two parts. Firstly we need to physically go to the shops, where we can initiate the reflection on gratitude. Secondly, we take the mental content from our shopping trip into the quiet of our meditation.

Take a trip to the shops; it could be a big supermarket where you do the weekly shop, or it could be going to get a few things from your local store. Alternatively, you can even do the shop online! However, this practice is more effective if you can go and see the actual products.

When you arrive, please take a look at the stock on the shelves. Think about where the items come from, even note the country of origin.

Many of the products you see will have been imported and transported from the other side of the world. Millions of people have been involved in you being able to benefit from and consume all your favourite foods; from those who planted, grew, and farmed your food, to those who packaged, transported and bought it, and finally to those who stocked the shelves from which you choose the food you would like.

As you shop gently reflect like this, and allow the experience of gratitude to naturally arise in your mind.

Not only will this reflection increase your happiness and appreciation as you shop but will also help you to keep a peaceful, calm, patient mind, which then acts as an antidote to the frustrations of trolley rage!

As you return from shopping to unpack, or as you have your shopping delivered, you can maintain the mind of gratitude. Gratitude is a habit of mind. If you are skilful with how you interact with your world, you can transform all your activities into a reflection on gratitude, which means that you can derive great enjoyment from the simplest of mundane activities like unpacking your shopping.

Not only will you be engaged in a physical activity, but you will be mixing your mind with this precious attitude.

...

When we go shopping without this type of reflection, it can seem that the food has just appeared by magic on our shelves. However, there is an endless chain of cause and effect in place for us to be able to enjoy all the food that we eat. Within this chain, countless people work exceptionally hard, although we can't see them. However, reflection on gratitude allows us to open our eyes to the world around us and see the 'invisible' kindness that we are continuously receiving. As a result, we start to see the reality clearly, and our mind naturally uplifts.

Not only is this a training in gratitude but we are also training in observing, training in noticing. Of course, the speed and distraction in our lives makes this challenging. It is, however, possible to slow down and see more, it just requires a decision. When we slow down and notice mindfully, we can see more than hard, physical objects. Within every object we can see an extensive network. With our mindful awareness we tap into this and allow gratitude to grow. We can make this happen anywhere. With a careful eye and a light heart guiding us, in the most domestic, unromantic, unexotic location, we can find peace, gratitude, and inspiration.

Please gently bring yourself into the present moment by focusing on the sensation of the breath entering and leaving your body.

Start to notice all the sensations in your body and allow your breath to heal the tension that has built up.

As you breathe in, mentally say to yourself:
Breathing in, I arrive in the present moment.

As you breathe out, mentally say to yourself:
Breathing out, I let go of any stress and distraction.

Engage with this for as long as you need to so your mind can settle and relax.

Start to reflect on the network of activity that you benefit from each day.

Consider the time that you went shopping and reflect on the kindness that you received.

Allow this contemplation to be positive and bring an experience of gratitude into your mind.

When gratitude arises clearly and fully, try to hold it with single-pointed concentration for as long as possible.

If your mind of gratitude fades, bring your attention to the sensation of your breath and try to refocus your mind.

When there is a little more focus, rekindle the mind of gratitude and try to become one with it, so that your mind and the experience of gratitude mix together, almost as though you become one with this emotion.

It is as though you are flavouring your mind with gratitude.

Enjoy this mixing process.

When you are ready to bring your meditation to a close, determine to carry the mind of gratitude with you into your everyday life.

...

Notes and Discussion

How can you remember the invisible 'kindness' chain in your activities?

Do you think that this remembrance will change the way that you shop?

How do you think the mind of gratitude will change your attitude towards those who serve you?

Can you imagine having gratitude for everything you encounter?

At the end of your day, write down five gratitudes.

Day 30

Breakfast: Starting the day right

With mindful eating we encourage ourselves to wake up from the auto-pilot mind that neutralises our thinking, functioning to make us feel that the everyday moments in our life are not worthy of our full attention due to our continual familiarity with them.

If we are mindful, we can regularly refresh our experience of connecting with the world as it actually is; being completely new, and changing from moment to moment.

If we can reflect on gratitude in a gentle, calm manner, our mind will become peaceful and uplifted, allowing a stream of great joy and peace to flow into our mind.

Just because we have engaged in an activity many times doesn't qualify it as being ordinary. An activity becomes ordinary if we engage with it while holding onto an ordinary mind. Learning to reflect on gratitude empowers us to take our mind out of the ordinary.

You can practise gratitude as you are preparing your breakfast, as you are enjoying eating it, as you are clearing everything away, or through the entire process. Alternatively, you can take a few moments at any point during the process to stop, pause and reflect.

For example, just before you eat your food you can stop and peacefully reflect:

How fortunate I am to enjoy this nourishing breakfast that can sustain me throughout the morning. Across the world, many are without food or are searching for food, right now. Many people worked tremendously hard for me to enjoy this food; how kind of them.

Briefly pause and cultivate the mind of appreciation and gratitude, then shine it upon your breakfast. Enjoy your breakfast and, if possible, try to retain the mind of gratitude as you are eating. This process of bringing gratitude into your mind is more natural if you slow down the way you eat, take your time, chew your food, and try not be in a rush to finish.

...

Many meditators will tell you that the optimum time of day to train in meditation is first thing in the morning; when our mind is at its freshest, giving us the precious opportunity to set our internal mental attitude for the day. Likewise, if we train in gratitude when taking our breakfast, we create a positive, mental opener for our day, thereby giving us the chance to maintain a stable, grateful mind. The attitude and intention that we choose to start the day with will determine the minds which arise throughout the day.

If we can start the day with gratitude, we open a positive door for subsequent uplifted states of minds to enter through. Everything comes from our intention, even as we are reading this, we can make the determination: *I am going to start my day with the positive mental attitude of gratitude.* This pure intention sows the seed for us to be able to accomplish this.

Having snacks through the day

If we snack, why not use this habit as a time to stop, pause, reflect and allow gratitude to flow into our life? When we mindfully snack, we create the habit to generate gratitude while we are on the go.

For this practice, stop what you are doing, and sit or stand where you can focus for a few minutes.

Take the snack and reflect on your good fortune for having access to this food.

Have a look at where the food has come from; whether it is from the other side of the world or grown in your own garden.

Think about the millions of people who have worked so hard to get this snack into your hands, or the effort that you yourself have put into its cultivation; and how being able to have this effort depends upon a network of other people's kindness.

If you allow yourself to think carefully, you can appreciate how it has arisen in dependence upon countless people.

Take several mindful breaths while reflecting on and appreciating the kindness that you have received from others, then with this grateful mind, enjoy the snack.

Upon completion, as you are about to finish, make the heartfelt determination to carry gratitude into the rest of your day.

...

Notes and Discussion

What morning routine can you use to remind you to bring gratitude to your breakfast table?

Can you graze with gratitude, how can you build this habit into your day?

At the end of your day, write down five gratitudes.

Day 31

Coffee: Wake up and smell it!

Using a drink bought from a shop (if you don't drink coffee then replace with your favourite beverage), now is our opportunity to not only enjoy our cup of coffee but to experience it mindfully, and use the moments as our time to develop gratitude. We can take the chance to practise as soon as we enter the shop. If we tend not to buy drinks outside, apply and adapt the instructions creatively to the drink that we have at home.

The kind servers who prepare your coffee for you came to work today and are working hard so you can enjoy your drink. As you are waiting for them to make your drink, reflect upon their kindness so you can enjoy your coffee. Hold this mind of gratitude while you are waiting. This attitude transforms your entire waiting experience into a grateful meditation, which you can apply to all the times that you wait for any form of service.

As your coffee arrives, thank the person who gave it to you, take it somewhere relatively quiet, and sit down. Pause, enjoy several mindful breaths, start to reflect where the coffee has come from and contemplate all those who have been involved in the harvesting and transportation of the beans so you can sit and enjoy; you can also reflect on the water, and the milk and sugar if you take them.

Reflecting carefully on your coffee, you can see that for you to enjoy this experience you depend upon an incredible network across the world. Pause briefly and remember. Develop gratitude and appreciation. Then enjoy the taste of your coffee. Try to carry gratitude in your mind as you enjoy your entire drink. You can even mentally say thank you as you are drinking the coffee.

As you are about to finish your drink make the intention to carry the mind of gratitude into the rest of your day.

...

Most importantly with our mindful training is to try to practise and not worry too much, we don't need to push and feel that we are doing something artificial; practise gently until we can have a natural experience.

When travelling in Laos, I took a trip to a coffee plantation. It was connected to a coffee shop in the town of Luang Prabang. The coffee shop was busy, popular with both locals and tourists from across the world for serving delicious tasting drinks and home-made delicacies, but also for selling fresh coffee beans from their plantation.

When we first sit in a coffee shop, it is rare to make a connection with the network of activity that leads to the coffee that we are drinking. Usually, we tend to focus on the ultimate outcome: the taste! And even then we can be distracted by other things in our life, preventing us from being fully present.

When I visited the Laos coffee shop, looking around, I could see many people just like myself involved in their daily activities while enjoying their coffee. It requires time, space, and reflection to bring gratitude into our experience. I tried to encourage this to grow by taking a visit to this coffee shop's plantation the following day, around a 35 km drive from the shop.

I took a step back from the busyness and got to see where the coffee had come from; its growth from a small seed and the extensive work that goes into getting the good quality beans into one's cup. As this was a small plantation, some of the sorting work was still carried out by hand, a painstaking process of quality control where each bean was hand-checked for size and colour by a group of workers sitting in the same positions all day.

It was a privilege and a real insight to see this process. When returning to the coffee shop and taking a coffee the next day, I was able to fully immerse myself in the invisible gratitude meditation of cause and effect. The coffee tasted even better by reflecting on the actions that were taken for me to be able to enjoy this delicious drink.

Through using our imagination and mindful awareness, we can try to remember the extensive network that we benefit from and thereby enrich all the moments in our life.

Notes and Discussion

How can you start to see the invisible network of kindness in the drinks that you enjoy daily?

Do you think that drinking with gratitude will increase the tastiness of the beverage that you are enjoying?

At the end of your day, write down five gratitudes.

Day 32

Preparation: It's all about the prep.

Today is our opportunity to train in gratitude while we are preparing our meal, adding the flavour of gratitude, and discovering how this secret ingredient can help our food have a delicious taste. Once again, we need to take our time and not rush. Try to notice all the sensations and smells, not speeding ahead of each task but just taking our time.

When you start to prepare your meal, remember the gratitude that you have been training in thus far and make the intention that through the preparation you are going to try to keep this attitude in your heart.

As you prepare your meal, stay in the present moment and think about all those who worked hard for you to have the food.

Consider how lucky you are to have food to prepare, and how this food can sustain your body so that you can have a happy and healthy life.

You can also reflect that you would be powerless to train your mind if you did not have this nourishing food.

Consider in this way and allow the mind of gratitude to develop in your heart.

If you are making the meal for someone reflect on the kindness that they have shown you and, as a way of repaying this, you are now preparing them a meal.

Try, if you can, to focus on one stage of the preparation at a time.

Consider where the ingredients have come from and the network of kindness that you find yourself within.

Although you are engaged in a physical act of movement, try to exercise mindful awareness, while at the same time keeping the precious mind of gratitude within your consciousness.

If your mind starts rushing ahead, getting frustrated, annoyed or overheated, pause, take a few breaths, bring gratitude to mind and come into the present moment, being led by your physical actions.

When your meal is ready, take the opportunity to serve it with gratitude in your mind.

...

A remarkable quality of the mind, depending upon its state, is the affect it can have on the taste of the food that we prepare. We can't see this secret ingredient with our eyes, but we can feel and taste it. Even if we initially don't believe this statement intellectually we can come to discover its truth from our own experience, by mindfully noticing and appreciating the tastes of the different foods that we eat.

When I was leading a mindful meditation retreat in Tuscany, members of the group commented continually on the delicious taste of the food. Yes, the retreat venue grew many of their ingredients organically in their grounds, and the environment of the Chianti district is blessed with some of the best temperate conditions in the world for grape cultivation, and yes they had a chef with many years' experience who cooked with great flair and confidence. However, there was something else. If we had met the staff and chef - we would see that they were cooking and preparing food in the kitchen with a happy, positive mind and, most crucial a good heart of gratitude and compassion; this was the secret ingredient. It is the same when we taste home cooking — our mother's or grandmother's cooking — there is nothing quite like it; not necessarily the refined taste, ingredients or complexities, but the heart, the positive energy and mind that goes into it.

If we can start to bring gratitude to play when we are preparing our food we will have discovered the secret ingredient for our recipes in the kitchen.

Notes and Discussion

Does preparing food with gratitude bring a new flavour to your dish?

How is it that your mind can affect the taste of the food that you eat?

At the end of your day, write down five gratitudes.

Day 33

Lunch: Take that break - you deserve it

It's time now for us to enjoy our lunch. To do this effectively we are going to need to take a proper lunch break, away from the usual distractions. It doesn't have to be for a long time, just enough time to allow us to generate the precious mind of gratitude.

We live in a culture that doesn't particularly value the lunch-break. In the workplace, it is common now for staff to not even take a break but to eat at their desks (desktop dining), eat during a meeting, eat while travelling, or eat while checking social media and emails on the phone. I have been told by students who attend my Mindful Eating class, which is taken from Chapter Six of the beginners' book, *Guide to the Mindful Way of Life,* that although they want to take a lunch break, they feel guilty for having one, expecting that somewhere down the line, if the lunch break habit continues, they will be penalised. In a sense, it can be an unwritten rule in the office - to not take a break, especially for food. Keep on working! Although, on the surface, not having breaks may seem advantageous for a company; with no encouragement to rest the mind, concentration can easily fade, tiredness and resentment can set in, and in the long run an entire workforce can deteriorate.

The culture whereby we work continually for as many hours as possible without a break leads to presenteeism. We are present at work, performing our duties, but potentially 50% absent due to distraction and mental fatigue, which has arisen from not taking enough breaks. As well as a gradual deterioration of the mind and our ability to focus, this distracted outlook can eventually affect the health in our body: our digestive, respiratory, and nervous systems.

It is a deep subject, and we could spend the rest of the book discussing it. Stepping back, it can be helpful to appreciate that distraction and busyness have become deeply ingrained within our culture to the point where if there is a person who is neither distracted or busy they will stand out, appear slightly unusual, and be potentially labelled as 'weird'.

If we wish to bring gratitude to play when we are having lunch, it needs to be done skilfully, gradually and deeply. The first step is making a plan. Consider before lunch time where we can have our lunch so we can allow ourself to generate this precious mind. It is possible of course to generate gratitude on the go, when we are busy. However, to give ourself the best opportunity, it can also be helpful to set aside time. To spend time organising our lunch, so we have space in our mind to cultivate this attitude.

For this practice, please focus on the actual moments when you are eating lunch.

When your lunch is ready, please place it in front of you.

Pause.

Mentally step back.

Take several mindful breaths.

Look gently at your food.

Reflect on how fortunate you are to have this nourishing food. There are many people in the world without food, experiencing starvation.

Reflect on the abundance that you have in your life.

Feel the good fortune in your heart rising in the aspect of the mind of gratitude. Try to carry this through your meal.

With this happy mind of gratitude, begin to eat.

Try, if you can, to hold gratitude through your lunch, taking your time and recognising your good fortune.

Pausing and digesting.

Chewing your food mindfully allows your body and mind to relax while eating, and creates the perfect environment to be able to hold the virtuous mind of gratitude in your heart.

Reflecting and allowing appreciation to arise continually.

Eating slowly and encouraging gratitude to remain.

At the end of your lunch, make a dedication that, as a result of the positive actions that have come from your gratitude practice, many people will have the opportunity to find nourishing food to sustain their life.

Determine not to take for granted the food that you enjoy on a daily basis.

...

Notes and Discussion

How can you start to create the time to have a grateful lunch?

Can you encourage this culture in your family and at work?

At the end of your day, write down five gratitudes.

Day 34

Supper: Winding down and recharging

Today, wind down with a mindful meal seasoned with gratitude. We sit down to have supper and reflect on gratitude while maintaining mindful awareness.

When your food is ready and in front of you, pause, take a few mindful breaths and think about where your food has come from, how it has most likely travelled from all corners of the planet.

Reflect how you are on the receiving end of this network of kindness.

Bring to mind the practices that you have engaged in thus far, so you recall the feeling of deep appreciation and gratitude.

When you train in gratitude, you are not just repeating that you are lucky and grateful; you are generating a genuine feeling of appreciation.

When gratitude comes to mind, try to hold it for as long as you can, either just at the beginning of your meal or if you can maintain your focus through the duration.

When you are starting with these practices, it helps to slow down your actions, to give yourself the time needed to allow gratitude to arise.

One way to slow down the process of eating is to chew your food and between mouthfuls to put your cutlery down while you eat.

As you chew your food more, the entire process of eating your meal will take longer. Usually, if you were eating in auto-pilot mode you could potentially become bored at this point and distract yourself. However, now you can take the opportunity to generate the precious mind of gratitude.

Determine at the end of your meal that you will carry the mind of appreciation and gratitude through the rest of your day and take it to bed with you.

It can be helpful when you have finished eating, instead of rising immediately, clearing up and going on to the next task, to pause, let your food digest, and once again cultivate gratitude for having the opportunity to enjoy this healthy meal.

...

Everyone's circumstance and journey are different and unique; the gratitude instructions given in this text are one way to practise. We can't necessarily practise like this straightaway. We can, however, engage in some of the trainings presented and cultivate a wish in the future to have space in our mind and life so that we can engage fully with the gratitude practices.

We all know the feeling of gratitude. When it arises, we naturally want to say thank you. Our heart warms and opens. In these practices, we are creating the conditions through the mind training exercises, so this precious attitude arises as often as possible.

Notes and Discussion

How can you bring gratitude to play in your family meal times?

Do you think that this one practice has the power to transform your relationships with your family and community?

At the end of your day, write down five gratitudes.

Day 35

Company: Harmony at mealtimes

When I lived in a Buddhist community, the principal teacher would emphasise the importance of harmony. To encourage this, we would stop each day at lunchtime, pause, breathe and eat together. However busy we were, we took the opportunity every day to spend quality time in each other's company. This was emphasised daily, year after year. It helped to strengthen and build connection and harmony.

If we live with our family or in a community, try to do this as often as you possibly can. Also we can try to add the gratitude practices detailed below, to make our mealtime even richer.

On this day take the opportunity to have a meal with somebody. If today we don't have this chance, wait and practise when the opportunity arises.

As you are reading this instruction, try to determine to engage with this practice next time you have a meal with somebody. Everything hinges on our intention and, if you can make this firm, you will find yourself having the time and mindspace to practise. To some degree, it involves multi-tasking, which you can do mindfully if you have enough determination and if you slowly pace yourself.

You are going to be eating, talking, and mixing the mind of gratitude with the entire experience. You may wish to wait until the end of your meal to discuss some of the more detailed points.

This gratitude practice can be anything; from you reflecting gently on the kindness of those whose company you are sharing all the way through to using the below points to start the gratitude discussion while you are together.

As you are enjoying the meal, reflect how fortunate you are to have company when you are eating.

You can think about the kindness you have received from the person whose company you now share.

If it is appropriate, you can discuss your experience of training in gratitude during the week with the person with whom you are sharing your meal.

You can do this either at the beginning of your meal for a few minutes, chat while you are enjoying your meal, or right at the end.

Notice what happens to your mind when you start talking about gratitude.

The incredible element of gratitude is that it is a natural human emotion and redirects our mind towards happiness.

If you discuss gratitude with someone in a natural way, the mood of the conversation uplifts and becomes positive.

As with all the training you are engaged in here, practise in accordance with your ability and that of the person with whom you are sharing your food with.

Discussion questions for your mealtime:

What do you feel grateful for in general?

What elements of this experience can help develop gratitude?

In what ways can gratitude help this relationship?

What do you feel most grateful for in your past?

What do you feel most grateful for right now?

What can you be grateful for in the future?

When your discussion comes to an end, reflect on how you can take your experience of gratitude into your life.

...

Notes and Further Discussion

How important is it for you to spend quality time eating with your loved ones?

Can grateful eating practices transform your relationships?

At the end of your day, write down five gratitudes.

Grateful Relationships

Meaningful interactions

...

In this next series of reflections, we build on the practices from previous weeks. In particular, we draw from week two, where we explored our grateful network. Now we take this practice deeper, generating gratitude for the opportunities and experiences that we have been given from the relationships in our life

Firstly, we reflect on our friends; initially from the past, to the friends that we have now, and finally the friends that we will have in the future. We then move our gratitude reflection to our teachers, to the family who are with us right now, to those who have come before us and, finally, to those who provide us with physical nourishment.

Throughout our life, we have had the fortune to have people who have provided company, companionship, empathy and affection. This week is our opportunity to shine the light of gratitude onto this, uplifting our mind, healing and enriching our interactions with others, and bringing happiness to the present moment

...

Day 36

Friends: Appreciating the support we receive

Today we can choose between two practices, or combine them together. First, we recall the friends from the past, then we recall both the friends we have now and those we will have in the future.

Friends (past): Remembering the kindness

In the first reflection, we scan back through our life. We are not dwelling or getting stuck in the past; we are fully present, but we use the experiences that we have had from the past to enhance our contemplations. We engage in the meditation with skill and focus so that we are not distracted by what happened; we try to just concentrate on the kindness that has been shown to us.

We can take a friend that we had, or we can make the contemplation more general when we bring in a series of friends. The friends that we have had in the past went out of their way for us, offering their time, giving us support, care, and attention. We reflect in a positive, uplifting way until our contemplation leads to an experience of gratitude and appreciation in our heart. When this mind arises clearly, we hold it with a relaxed single-pointed concentration. We try to mix our attention thoroughly with gratitude so that our mind becomes one with this precious emotion.

Please sit in a relaxed, upright posture, with your back straight and shoulders dropped, letting go of any tension in the upper-half of your body.

Gather your attention into the present moment.

Notice the contact between your body and the floor beneath you.

Allow your mind to settle into the present moment.

Bring your attention to the complete sensation of your breath. Notice the warm feeling at the tip of your nostrils as you breathe in and the cool sensation as you breathe out.

As you breathe in, adjust and straighten your posture slightly. As you breathe out, allow any tension in your shoulders and face to drop.

When your mind is relatively focused, begin your contemplation.

Bring a friend or group of friends from the past to mind.

Reflect:

I have experienced great kindness from friends that I have had in the past. They gave me their time, attention, and generosity.

Bring to mind and recall a friend, and reflect on the kindness that they have shown you. Try to be specific with your practice so that you can make it heartfelt.

Contemplate in a gentle, relaxed, focused way, until the experience of gratitude dawns in your heart. When the mind of gratitude rises, try to calmly-abide with it — single-pointedly — for as long as possible.

Moment by moment, abide with gratitude.

If your mind becomes distracted or starts to wander off, use your breath to bring your grateful attention to the present. Return to the contemplation and recall your experience again.

Practice for as long as you can.

As your practice is about to conclude, determine to carry gratitude into the rest of your life and integrate it with your interactions with others.

We start to establish the habit so that when we think about our friends from the past we develop gratitude for the kindness that they have shown us. Instead of thinking about what they should have done or could have done we think about what they *have* done.

We will explore in more detail the challenging relationships that we have had in Chapter Seven, where we look at the theme of grateful adversity. For the time being, at this stage, we take the time to appreciate the relationships that have enriched our lives.

Friends (present and future): Opening our grateful eyes

In this training, we use a similar process of contemplation as explained in the previous practice, but now we adapt it for the friends whom we currently have in our life.

If, at this moment, there is nobody who comes to mind then reflect on those friends whom you could potentially have. Within this world, there are countless opportunities for cultivating, increasing and growing our friendships.

Find a quiet place to reflect, and sit in a relaxed, upright posture, establishing a stable connection with the ground beneath you.

Gently bring your attention to the present moment and gently close your eyes.

If you feel tired, allow your eyes to open slightly and gaze at a small point on the floor in front of you.

Allow your body and mind to relax gradually; there is no rush, take your time, enjoying the opportunity you have made for yourself.

Bring your attention to the sensation of the breath; try to become one with the process for a short time.

When your mind is relatively focused, begin your contemplation. If you wish you can recall a friend and reflect on the kindness that they show you, even imagining them next to you.

I experience great kindness from the friends that I have now and those I will have in the future. They give me their time, attention, and generosity.

Contemplate in a gentle, relaxed, focused way until the experience of gratitude comes: a warm, positive, uplifted feeling in your heart. When the mind arises, try to hold it with single-pointed concentration.

From moment to moment, calmly-abide with this mind.

If your mind becomes distracted or wanders from the object of meditation, use your breathing to bring your attention to the present moment.

Return to the contemplation and recall your experience again.

Enjoy the opportunity to practice and engage in this positive reflection for as long as possible.

As your practice concludes, determine to carry your experience into the rest of your life. Determine, when you are with your friends, to try and develop gratitude for the kindness that they show you.

...

If we can develop gratitude for our friends, our relationships with them will improve, and we open the door for new, positive interactions in the future. With a positive outlook and approach to life, we will naturally attract this. What we decide to put into the world with our mind, body and speech, will naturally return to us.

One helpful view we can take into the world concerning our friendships is to regard ourself as a potential friend to anyone who needs one. With this blissful attitude, our mind and heart will be open, positive and full of gratitude.

Notes and Discussion

What benefits come from positively looking to your past?

Does it help to remember the past, or should you just let it go?

How can you learn to appreciate someone from the past if they didn't recognise us?

How can you show the mind of gratitude to the friends in your life?

Do you think that generating gratitude for a friend when you are not with them enhances the relationship?

How can you hold gratitude in your mind while communicating with others?

At the end of your day, write down five gratitudes.

Day 37

Teachers: Reflecting on those who show the way

We consider the teachers who have appeared in our life; from parents, guardians and elders, who taught us our first words, and primary teachers who helped us learn to read, write and calculate, through to teachers in our later education, who taught us more complex reasoning, skills and understanding.

When we finished school to go home and play, teachers were left to carry on, preparing and marking our work, potentially taking our work home with them to mark in the evening and at the weekend. We may never have considered this while at school.

Everything we currently know how to do, we have been shown how to do by someone. Even if we think we have taught ourself an activity, we have still depended on others who have taught us the basic skills to be in that privileged position to evolve.

Someone once showed us how to hold a pen, how to feed ourself, how to sit on a bike, how to turn on a computer, how to turn on a stove, how to turn on a car. As a result of their kindness we can move forward and enjoy our life.

Later in the text we consider the hidden teachers who help us practise patience. Here we highlight those teachers who have taught and shared their knowledge with us, empowering us to be the person who we are today. In our reflection, we can also consider our lineage of teachers, our teachers' teachers and those who have come before them.

We can also bring to mind those who have taught us by their example, whether they knew that is what they were doing or not. Teaching by example is the most powerful way to deliver a message, and perhaps there have been people in our lives who have inspired us through their example to make changes and move into a happier place.

We reflect on the kindness we have received from the teachers who have come into our life, and allow a mind of gratitude to arise in our heart. When gratitude arises calmly-abide with it, from moment to moment.

Please bring your attention into the present moment.

Listen in a relaxed way to the sounds around you.

Gather your awareness into your body.

Notice the sensations in your body.
In particular, the rising and falling of your breath.

Start to notice how your breath enters and leaves your body.

Locate the cool sensation at the tip of the nostrils as you breathe in and the warm sensation as you breathe out. Focus on this for a while.

When your mind is relaxed and gathered, begin to engage in the gratitude reflection. You could imagine the teachers in your life next to you, to make the meditation more powerful.

I have had many teachers throughout my life. They have empowered me to possess all the skills and abilities that I currently have. If I use all that I have learned from others, not only can I find happiness in my life but I can also be of great service to my community. How kind of all my teachers to have worked so hard to provide me with this knowledge.

We reflect in this way for a short time, trying to make the contemplation personal and heartfelt. As a result of this reflection, when the mind of gratitude arises, try to hold it single-pointedly for as long as possible.

If the mind fades, or you find it challenging to concentrate due to distraction, use the mindspace motivation:

Breathing in - *I generate gratitude and remember the kindness that I have received from others.*

Breathing out - *I let go of all the distraction and tiredness in my mind.*

Abide with gratitude for as long as you possibly can.

When it is time to bring your session to a close, make the intention to carry gratitude into your daily life and not to forget the kindness that you have received from your teachers.

...

Notes and Discussion

How many teachers in your life can you remember who have shown you kindness? Bring them to mind. Talk about them. List them.

How can you repay the kindness you have received from the teachers that you have met?

Bring to mind five gratitudes from the day.

Day 38

Family: Finding peace with those closest

In this reflection, we develop gratitude and appreciation for those in our family who have shown us kindness; this can include both those from the past and present. This practice can consist of both blood relatives and those who have played a significant part in our growth.

These reflections are designed to bring a positive warmth and openness into our subjective experience. As with the previous grateful friend contemplations, it may be that our relationships with those in our life have at times been challenging and complex. We will look further into this in Chapter Seven, Grateful Adversity. For the sake of these practices we focus and direct our attention towards the obvious positives. We can use anyone from our family; for example, we can use our parents.

They gave us the body that we now inhabit. All the richness of our life only comes as a result of them having decided to provide us with life. It was a miraculous experience to be born. We were allowed into this world and provided with shelter, protection and nourishment, only due to our parents.

Reflecting gently and positively in this way, we let the mind of gratitude and appreciation to arise. We only need to contemplate and reflect until the mind of gratitude arises; when it does, we try to mix our mind with this positive mental attitude.

We can reflect on the kindness of our parents having given us this life. Alternatively, we can consider a particular act of generosity that someone in our family showed us. We can alternate between different contemplations each time we engage in the practice. We can work through various members of our family, with the result being that a mind of gratitude arises. We mix our mind with it so there is no separation between our mind and gratitude. It is almost as though we become the mind of gratitude.

Sitting in a relaxed upright posture, please bring your attention into your body.

Allow your body and mind to settle into the moment.

Bring your attention to the sensation of the breath and start to count the out-breath.

See if you can gently count ten rounds of natural exhalations, several times.

When your mind is relatively focused, begin your gratitude contemplation.

Reflect on the body that you currently enjoy and all the experiences that you have had due to being given this life.

These arise due to our parents. Allow your mind to flash back to kindnesses you have received. This first relationship meant that you can now enjoy this life.

Contemplate and reflect in a relaxed, focused way until gratitude arises clearly in your mind; when it does try to mix your attention with it single-pointedly.

To stay engaged, use your breath as an anchor to guide you to the present moment.

As your practice concludes, determine to carry the experience into the rest of your life so when you think of your family members, gratitude arises clearly.

...

Notes and Discussion

How can you show the mind of gratitude to your family?

Can gratitude heal your family relationships?

At the end of your day, write down five gratitudes.

Day 39

Ancestors: Diving into the richness of our history

Today we reflect on our family from the past. We begin with our grandparents and take our reflection further into our ancestry. In meditation, we see how far back our mind can go with the precious mind of gratitude.

We may already have a clear knowledge of those in our family tree and remember relationships with grandparents and even great-grandparents. Bring these to mind. If you do not know your grandparents consider them in the abstract, or with just the details that you have been told in that they are the people who brought your parents into being.

We are only able to enjoy this life due to our ancestors, and these go back continually. In the reflection we let our mind travel as far as possible, with the sole intention to reflect on the kindness that our previous family showed by having and looking after their children. We are the product of this kindness.

Without careful consideration, we may think that they didn't show us any kindness; however, with a positive mental attitude, we can see that we now benefit directly from our ancestors. Without them we would not have an existence; therefore, we can say that we have received enough from them to now be able to cultivate gratitude and appreciation.

We highlight our attention on what the people in our life have done, as opposed to focusing on what they haven't. In this way, the focus of our attention provides us with the basis and correct content for the cultivation of gratitude.

If we allow our mind to be influenced strongly by indifference we will not highlight how we exist due to the kindness of others; we will create the habit of relating to others in a way that only sees them through the filter of what they can do for us, and thereby appreciation is blocked from arising within.

For gratitude to arise, it is important to have our attention focusing on the parts of our life, which act as a foundation for the growth of mental attitude. We try to establish the habit of considering what we receive from others in our relationships, not what we don't or should receive from them. Let us try meditating on this theme.

Try to engage with this practice for as long as you can, finding a quiet, relaxed place to sit. Ideally, a location that is well ventilated, has natural daylight and is free from distraction.

Sitting in a relaxed upright posture, bring your attention into your body. Let yourself settle into the present moment.

Notice the sensation of your breath.

Imagine that each time you breathe in you inhale positive energy, and each time you breathe out you let go of any negative, anxious energy.

When you feel relatively focused, begin your contemplation. Allow your mind to reflect on your ancestors. Reflect on their kindness.

Think of the body that you are currently residing in, allow the appreciation to dawn that this is only here because of the kindness of your ancestors who have come before you.

See how far your mind can go back in meditation, bringing to mind those from your family whom you can remember, or know of, and allowing the recognition to dawn that their lives depended upon their family and grandparents, ad infinitum.

Contemplate in this way until gratitude arises clearly within your consciousness. When it does, mix your attention with it so you become one with this precious mind.

Try, in the quiet of meditation, to hold gratitude for as long as you possibly can.

When the practice comes to its natural conclusion, decide in your heart to carry the experience into the rest of your day and life.

...

As a result of engaging in this training, when we reflect on our personal history, we allow gratitude to arise in our mind. In some Confucian, Tao, and Pagan traditions, they have shrines devoted to their ancestors. Each day they offer remembrance and respect for those who have gone before them, even offering food and water in front of their images; generating the mind of gratitude as they do so.

There may be pictures of our family in our house, in a similar way to these ancient traditions we can take the opportunity to generate gratitude when we seem them.

There may be a particular time we can set to visit the grave, or area where our loved one's ashes have been scattered, where we stop, reflect on the kindness that person has shown us, and determine to make the very most of the time that we have left on this planet, in loving memory of them.

Notes and Discussion

How can you learn to reflect on gratitude as you think about your ancestors?

What do you think about creating an ancestor shrine in your house?

At the end of your day, write down five gratitudes?

Day 40

Chefs: Gratitude for those who sustain us

In today's contemplation, we consider the relationships which have sustained and nourished our physical body. In particular, we can spend time reflecting on the food that has been cooked for us. Perhaps today, this week, this month, this year.

When we are at a restaurant or cafe there is often little chance to directly interact with those who cook for us. The chefs are usually hidden away, working in a kitchen so those in the restaurant can enjoy their food, but it can be hot, hard work. In our reflection, we can also include the factory kitchens across the world, which produce pre-prepared food that is consumed across the planet every day. We may not have seen or contemplated the hidden kindness in our world that we are on the receiving end of, unless we have worked in such places.

We think of the meals cooked for us when we were a child, both by our family and the cooks in nursery, school, and college. Hundreds and thousands of meals cooked to help sustain our existence, so we have a healthy body and are able to enjoy our life. Many of these meals we may have just wolfed down, perhaps with little thought or reflection for the people who prepared the food.

Our connection to those who cook for us is a vital relationship we have. Although this relationship is hidden, it is there. We take the opportunity today to remember the kindness we have received from these chefs in the past, present, and future; and all the meals they have cooked and will cook for us.

We only exist today as a result of being sustained by this kindness. Even now, as you read these words, the food inside us, that gives us the energy to read these words, comes as a result of others' kindness.

Gratitude contemplation is extremely grounding and humbling. When we pause, reflect, breathe and step back from our ego, letting the awareness of others' kindness arise, naturally, gratitude manifests, allowing our mind to focus and uplift.

Please bring your attention into your body, sitting in a relaxed upright posture.

Allow your body and mind to settle into the present moment.

Bring your attention to the sensation of the breath. Begin to count the out-breath and try to count ten exhalations, several times.

As you breathe in, allow your mind to become relaxed and focused. As you breathe out, let go of any heaviness in your body and mind.

When your mind is relatively gathered, begin your contemplation.

Reflect on the food that has been cooked for you, perhaps today, this week, last month. Allow your mind to go back through your life in a focused, relaxed way.

Contemplate the kindness of those who have cooked for you, and the benefit you have received.

Skilfully allow gratitude and appreciation to arise naturally within your mind.

Bring your attention to the present moment with the mind of gratitude.

Although we initially go to the past to contemplate, we come into the present and focus, calmly-abiding with this precious mind.

Close your eyes for a short time and allow gratitude to well up inside you.

Stay with this experience of gratitude, as though your mind mixes completely with it and you become one with this emotion.

Use your breathing to concentrate.

If you become distracted, use your breath to help you return to the present moment.

If you find it challenging to stay focused, or your mind is very distracted, as you breathe in, you can say to yourself:

Breathing in, I allow gratitude to arise in my heart.

As you breathe out, you can say to yourself:

Breathing out, I let go of all distraction and negativity.

Once you have established your concentration, bring gratitude back into your consciousness and try to abide with it.

When you are ready to naturally conclude your practice, make the decision that you will turn on your gratitude radar when you are being cooked for, and integrate this reflection into your everyday life.

Try to put this intention into practise and see first-hand the positive effects of this training.

...

One of my teachers from the Buddhist temple that I lived in used to talk about how, in today's world, we have a critical radar that can always be looking out for others' faults and limitations. Here we are developing a gratitude radar that is actively seeking the kindness that we are receiving from others. We establish a grateful habit in our mind.

Just like any habit this takes time, but we have to make a start. I often say in the live classes that I teach, when someone mentions that they find the training challenging or difficult, to try and make it easy for themselves.

We can do this by not expecting great results straight away but rather breaking our mind training down into bite-size portions, so that at least we can encourage ourselves and make a start. If we expect too much, or wish to see instant change, this is a recipe for disappointment and discouragement. The key is to make a start. This can be for just one second a day. The next day two seconds, the next day three. After sixty days, this is one minute of grateful practice. Instead of discouraging yourself, encourage yourself and allow your mind to become positive, light and joyful.

Notes and Discussion

How can you remember to bring gratitude into your mind when you are being cooked for, when at that time you can't see this kindness directly?

If your mind becomes hardened when you are with others, how can you use gratitude to soften your experience?

At the end of your day, write down five gratitudes.

Day 41
The Hidden Service: Looking into our network

If we reflect on our relationships carefully, in the positive, peaceful space of meditation, gratitude can naturally arise.

We have countless physical, verbal, and mental interactions with others. All of these relationships can provide us with the chance to develop gratitude. Considering the network of our relationships helps us appreciate that we are continuously receiving benefit from other people's hard work. The kindness we receive from others is unceasing. By turning on our gratitude radar we can awaken this insight and, consequently, its influence will uplift and transform our mental state during daily life.

Take the chair you are currently sitting on, or if you are standing or lying down apply this reflection to the floor or bed:

Somebody designed the chair.

It was then constructed and assembled for you.

For this to happen, raw materials were required.

These were grown, harvested, manufactured, cut, picked, chosen, transported and bought.

All those involved in this process would amount to millions of people.

Consider that they were only able to do their work due to the food that they bought and were nourished by, which was planted and grown by someone who had a family, who had ancestors.

There is a network which we are currently a part of, and can't escape from, which involves countless people. All the people within this network are all working on our behalf, in the sense that we receive continuous benefit from their actions. If, in meditation, we allow our mind to enter this network in a positive, open, non-judgmental manner, and enjoy reflecting on this interaction, the gentle, positive, soft heart of gratitude can seamlessly arise.

Gratitude can emerge when we provide ourself with the time each day to step back from the pushing and busyness, and have the mindspace to wake up to the world around us. We are all interconnected. It is fair to say that we are 'in a relationship' of some sort with all the countless people who are in our network. With a focused and positive reflection, and with careful attention, we can awaken to this relationship and the connection that we have with everyone across the entire planet. The separation and division between 'us' and 'them' is fabricated by a one-dimensional view of the world.

For this practice, you will need to sit on a chair. Please bring your attention into your body and sit in a relaxed upright posture. Allow your body and mind to settle into the present moment.

Bring your attention to the sensation of your breath, and engage with its natural process.

When your mind is relatively focused, begin your contemplation. Reflect on the incredible network that you are intimately connected with.

Take an object like the chair on which you sit.

Consider: Who put the chair there? Who purchased it? Who transported it? Who made it? Who designed it? Who brought the different materials together? We can break down each of the elements and where they came from and all the people who were involved in that process.

Then there is the history and evolution of the chair, dating back to ancient Egypt over five thousand years ago. The chair on which we sit depends upon a wonderful, rich lineage, and we must remember within this history that people have worked incredibly hard, and the result of this for us now is the chair that we can sit on and relax in.

Each stage of the chair's evolution depends on other people. For example, the transportation required roads, which depended on people to design and build those roads, and for them to be able to do this, they depended on many other people in their lives.

As you reflect on an object such as the chair that your body now has physical contact with, you can start to gently allow your mind to expand and connect with the interconnectedness of your own experience.

Try to allow this understanding to bring about a heartfelt mind of gratitude and try to mix your attention with this single-pointedly.

Experience the incredible interconnectedness of your experience and try to absorb your mind into this. Consider the network that you are part of, and allow the mind of gratitude to arise for all the benefit that you directly experience from others.

When the mind of gratitude arises within your consciousness, try to focus on it with single-pointed concentration.

As your practice comes to a natural conclusion, resolve to take this mind of gratitude and the appreciation of the hidden service that you receive, into your daily life. If you are able to shine the light of gratitude on your experience, you can awake to the network with which you are intimately connected.

...

This practice is incredibly powerful in both helping us to reduce our feeling of isolation and melt away our sense of entitlement.

We can grow as an individual but feel completely isolated from the world around us. We can see across the world a growth in the number of people experiencing mental health issues, many stemming from an increased sense of meaninglessness and separation, leading to loneliness and unhappiness. We can feel as though we owe nothing to the world, but that it owes us; 'strangers' are not to be talked to but treated as suspicious and deceptive.

If we have had challenging moments with others, over time, as a mechanism to protect ourselves, we can start to harden our heart. As a consequence, our mind closes down to the opportunity to develop an appreciation for what we receive from others and obstructs any potential new relationships, obscuring our previous relationships and hardening our existing relationships.

Gratitude meditation provides us with a lens through which to view our world, encouraging warmth and a friendly attitude within our heart. We come to have a stable foundation for cultivating the minds of love and compassion, helping us erode our false, self-centred perspective, and providing us with an expansive, wholesome view of the world and those residing in it.

Notes and Discussion

How far can you reflect on the interconnected web that you are part of?

Can you take another object other than the chair and reflect on its evolution, to allow you to generate the mind of gratitude?

At the end of your day, write down five gratitudes.

Day 42

Servers: Opening to daily kindness

We finish our contemplations from the week with a reflection and meditation on the service that we receive each day. We are re-visiting this practice, as we looked at it earlier in the book, due to the importance of the reflection and how it can enhance the gratitude meditation; here we go again!

Remember the gratitude mantra? We breathe in and reflect on our good fortune; we breathe out and reflect on the kindness of others. To make it easier, we engage in the following short practice.

Sit quietly and allow your body and mind to settle.

Start to focus on your breathing and let go of any nervous, busy, tense energy. As you focus on your breath, say to yourself:

Breathing in, I become gratitude.

Breathing out, I awaken to others' kindness.

Engage with this process for as long or as short as you wish, from a few moments or a few minutes, to a few hours, according to your wish and intention.

...

These two reflections will strengthen our gratitude. It is easy to miss the service we receive from others, to dismiss, and feel that we are entitled to it. With careful contemplation, we discover that others are continually serving us.

In the USA it is traditional for members of the public, when they see those from the armed forces, to thank them for their service to the country, to show appreciation and gratitude. With this reflection, we generate this attitude towards as many people as we can include in our mind, for the service that we are on the receiving end of in helping us enjoy our life.

For example, as I am writing this, I am sitting in a café. I have received services from those who prepared my lunch and coffee; outside, workers are paving the road to make it smooth and comfortable to walk on. There is a hotel across the way where there is a team of staff working to make the hotel clean and accommodating if I wish to stay there. When I use these services, I have a relationship with these people who worked hard to provide them. I can reflect, *'how kind that they are working so hard for my well-being and comfort'*.

Wherever we are right now, we can see there are many people around us working for our benefit. We receive so much as a result of the service from others. We take the time today to reflect on this. This contemplation is very practical; we can integrate it into our daily life. When we are travelling around, working and relaxing, we depend on the service of others; how much kindness we receive continually! Engage with the practice below for approximately ten minutes. We can make it longer or shorter, depending on our schedule. Alternatively, we can simply read it slowly and allow ourself to generate the gentle mind of gratitude.

Please bring your attention into your body, while sitting in a relaxed, upright posture.

Allow your body and mind to settle into the present moment.

As you breathe in, let your posture straighten. As you breathe out, let go of any stress or tension that may have built up.

Bring your attention to the complete sensation of your breath.

Begin to count the out-breath. Count ten exhalations, several times.

When your mind is relatively focused, begin your contemplation.

I have a multitude of relationships in my life; many of them are not obvious. I receive continuous benefit from other people The service and kindness that I have received from others is incalculable.

Reflect and allow the mind of gratitude and appreciation to arise. When gratitude arises in your mind, try to hold it single-pointedly.

If the mind fades, return to the contemplation or use your breath to refocus the mind.

Calmly-abide with the mind of gratitude for as long as possible. You can also use the grateful mantra to bring your attention to the present:

Breathing in, I become gratitude.

Breathing out, I awaken to others' kindness.

As your practice comes to a natural conclusion, decide to integrate your experience into your everyday life.

Try to be on the look-out for the service that you receive from others and the kindness that they have shown you.

...

Whether we choose to acknowledge it or not, the relationships in our life are everything; the quality of them governs our wellbeing and whether we can be happy.

Bringing and encouraging the mind of gratitude in relation to our interactions with everyone in our life will make them more meaningful, satisfying and engaging. As a result, not only will our mind be uplifted but the lives of those around us will be positively affected, resulting in harmony within our society.

The power of one person with a grateful mind should not be underestimated. They can make a significant difference in our world.

If we are unhappy with the world that we reside in, instead of allowing our energy to be dissipated by blaming people, organisations, institutions and governments, we direct our energy inwards, towards a positive, grateful path of mental transformation.

We encourage ourself to utilise the power that we have within our mind by channelling it into generating gratitude. Instead of our mental energy being drained by negative thinking, blaming externals conditions, it is protected and increased. Gradually as our training progresses, we will gain a subjective experience, that, with our mind, we create our world.

Notes and Discussion

What is your conclusion from spending a week thinking about the relationships in your life?

How can you now integrate this into your everyday experience?

At the end of your day, write down five gratitudes.

Grateful Adversity

Encouraging mental strength and resilience

Thus far, we have explored how to develop gratitude for our life experiences and enjoyments. We have noticed our good fortune, learned to increase our mental peace using the mind of gratitude during our daily activities, enhanced and strengthened our connection with our family and friends, and appreciated the incredible network of kindness we are linked to. These reflections and meditations act as a stable foundation for our gratitude training.

Human life, however, is challenging. Each day we have to encounter circumstances we don't wish for and potentially interact and communicate with people who challenge us. Generally, when our life is challenging and difficult, and we experience stress and anxiety, we don't naturally develop gratitude. It can be enough for us just to make it through the day and arrive in our bed to physically recover during our sleep.

Over time if we are not attentive and proactively train our mind, our default response can be to harden to the world and the people around us. This approach protects and secures our ego-centric view; if we maintain this view it becomes quite a challenge to open and initiate positive mental attitudes towards whatever arises in life. It can seem, through the filter of this perspective, that if we take the gratitude option, we will become vulnerable and be in a position within our life where people will have the opportunity to take advantage of us.

To be able to develop gratitude when life 'throws us lemons' requires having a thoroughly trained mind. We can learn to transform the difficulties life throws at us and use them to our advantage so we can increase our well-being and happiness. We can transform the lemons into lemonade or, as I said on a recent retreat in Italy, limoncello!

Through training in the practices contained in this chapter, we can start to become familiar with integrating, practising, and applying the mind of gratitude when challenges arise.

One helpful analogy is that adversities are like waves arising in the ocean of our life. Just as it is inevitable for waves to arise from an ocean, so it is unavoidable that we will have to endure challenges. If we have no knowledge of surfing and attempt to surf for the first time, we will struggle if we try to surf the big waves, and not enjoy the process. However, if we learn how to surf, when the waves of adversity rise we can learn to ride the waves. Just like a surfer who rises to the challenge of the big waves, and eventually goes in search of them, we can start to enjoy waves and finally recognise that the bigger the waves the more fun we can have riding them.

We can come to derive great satisfaction and confidence from learning to ride the waves of life and not be fazed, dragged down, or discouraged by the trials and tribulations of human existence.

Please note that this chapter will address some of the more challenging themes in human life; read with care. If you don't feel ready to work through these pages, return to the previous training to increase your resilience.

Day 43

Adversity: Creative, positive perspectives

Nobody wakes in the morning and wishes for adversity, but whether we like it or not, throughout our life we will have to endure unwished-for external and internal difficulties. Finally, we will have to deal with ageing, sickness and our life ending; this is before living through the ageing, sickness and death of those who we hold dear.

Many of the challenging issues that we must encounter in our life are things that we choose not to contemplate, so we don't talk about them. Of course, this doesn't prevent the issues from arising, it just postpones having to reflect on them. When they eventually do occur, we can feel surprised, shocked and depressed.

The good news is that we have the potential to transform this inevitable adversity. Just as weightlifters can learn to lift through consistent training and focus, beginning with the light weights and over time increasing their capability, so can we start to transform adverse conditions in our life. Over time, with training, we can increase our capability. To have success with this practice, we need to have a realistic perspective of our abilities and start with small adversities.

The first step is developing an understanding of our human situation. This reflection, if misunderstood, will, of course, depress the spirit. However, if we approach this contemplation with wisdom, the practice uplifts and stabilises our mind. We reflect how it is inevitable that, as a human, we are going to experience problems and difficulties; there is no way that we can avoid this. Whatever we choose to do, wherever we go, we can't hide from adversity; this is one of the characteristics of our human life.

We will have to encounter circumstances and situations that we would prefer not to. We will have to be parted from those that we love. In our life, we have to continually tolerate an underlying uncertainty about our situation, however secure and stable we have seemingly made our life.

With a relaxed, calm mind, we reflect on these points and arrive at an acceptance that our life will bring adversity, perhaps today, tomorrow, next week, next year ... we don't know when, but it is guaranteed! Reflecting with a peaceful mind allows a stability to arise within; an acceptance. Also, an insight that, when adversity does come, we have the potential, if we have trained our mind, to be able to respond with a creative, positive perspective.

We finish the practice with the determination to train our mind and increase our mental strength daily throughout our life.

It is important to take our time with these reflections. As our wisdom develops, we acclimatise to the content and can reflect with mindspace, consequently gaining wisdom and insight.

Please bring your attention to the present moment.

Mindfully listen to the sounds around you and gather your attention inwards.

Listen gently to the natural sound of your breathing.

Let go of the busyness in your mind. Allow your thoughts to slow down and your mind to focus.

As you breathe in, allow the mind of gratitude to arise for your breath and the life you currently enjoy.

As you breathe out, take the opportunity to release your mind from stress and anxiety.

Gently reflect on how you have had to experience adversity already in your life and that, in the future, you will have to endure further adversity and a myriad of different challenges. Reflect how this is inevitable:

It is because I am a human being that I must endure this. However I choose to design and arrange my life, adversity will come. My reputation, status, wealth and relationships not only can't protect me from adversity but can function to increase it.

Please determine to accept the nature of your human life and allow a stability of mind to arise. Abide with this for as long as possible.

After some time has passed, encourage the mind of gratitude to arise for having this opportunity to stabilise your mind.

When you decide to bring your session to a close, dedicate all the good energy from your practice so that you can carry stability of mind into your daily life.

...

An acceptance, appreciation and understanding that adversity will arise in our life is far from negative thinking; it is a realistic approach to the realities of human life and functions as a foundation for being able to develop a deeper form of gratitude in subsequent meditations.

The first words of Buddha himself when he started teaching were that you should understand suffering. He taught this to his followers to help them appreciate the realities of their existence, so that they could experience an authentic, genuine happiness; he didn't explain this to make his students miserable, far from it. If we can only be happy when we think about and experience 'nice things' then our happiness and contentment will be limited.

...

Notes and Discussion

How can you skilfully think about adversity in your life so you can generate a positive mind?

How can you overcome the mind that thinks, 'oh this is morbid', when discussing such issues?

At the end of your day, write down five gratitudes.

Day 44

Problem: Transforming our view

In this session, we reflect on exactly what is a 'problem,' and look at how we can inspire our mind to transform a situation by changing our view. It is helpful to recognise where the root of the problem is. If we respond to a challenging circumstance in our life with a negative mind, we create a problem. If we can learn to relate to the arising circumstance with a peaceful, positive, grateful mind, we may still have a challenging situation, but there is no inner problem.

Are they problems or challenges?

> Our train is late.
>
> Our car breaks down.
>
> We open a letter and discover a fine.
>
> Our bicycle tyre gets a puncture.
>
> We receive criticism.
>
> We are ignored.
>
> The dentist tells us that we need a filling.
>
> The doctor informs us of an illness.
>
> Somebody criticises us.
>
> We lose our position or status.
>
> We feel humiliated.
>
> We find ourselves in an unfair situation.
>
> We lose our phone, our wallet, or any personal items.
>
> Our possessions are stolen.
>
> An inanimate object is not working correctly.
>
> We have to wait (again) in a queue or traffic jam.

Yep, the list is endless! Are they problems or challenges?

Choose a circumstance in your life right now that appears as though it is causing you a problem. Consider if you feel there would be any way that you could change the internal reaction and response that you have towards it.

The one sure way to change the activity within our mind is by changing our view; we can empower ourself to do this by changing our mind. If we can learn to change our view of a circumstance, then we can start to transform it. If our mind changes, our world begins to change. Witnessing this process can bring great confidence to our mind.

Many times in our life, it can seem that we are powerless to the circumstance. It can feel as though there is nothing we can do to change what is happening. We may try to manipulate and alter the external conditions in our life to try and improve the situation; this can work temporarily, but it can also function to create new difficulties and problems.

The foundation for changing our view is by developing a peaceful mind in meditation and learning to accept the situation.

Let us take someone who has started experiencing discontent due to seeing their body ageing. As our body ages, changes occur. Through witnessing this, we may be unable to accept it and take a decision to have some form of surgery to encourage our youthful appearance to return. We can have surgery; for a while, this will alter our appearance and potentially our view of ourself. Along with this surgery though, there may also be side effects, expense and new issues that we must come to deal with. We can try and solve the 'problem' of the stress of seeing our body ageing by changing the external circumstances and, as a consequence, unintentionally bring on more adversity for ourself.

Another way to deal with adversity is by learning to change our mind, accepting the process of ageing as a natural happening in our life. Instead of fighting the process and pretending that it isn't happening, we accept it. With this patience and acceptance our mind becomes beautiful and peaceful, thus naturally altering our external appearance and bringing beauty to our body, from having a positive outlook. No amount of surgical work that we have on our external features will withstand our mind when it becomes negative and unhappy.

With the mind of acceptance, we can ask the questions in the quiet of meditation:

What would this situation feel like if I was to think about it with gratitude?

Could I solve this situation by changing my mind?

When we train in meditation, we start to give ourself the confidence to see that we can change our mind and, through changing our mind, the world around us alters. We can affect something that is currently happening by changing our attitude towards it; by changing our view. This knowledge is very empowering and can give us tremendous energy to make changes within.

Spend a few minutes bringing your attention into the present moment, directing your attention to your breathing in a relaxed, calm and focused manner.

Allow thoughts of the past and the future to dissolve into the present moment.

Take an open look at your mind and let your thoughts and distractions pass.

Then bring your attention to an issue that you are currently experiencing.

Ask yourself in the quiet of meditation:

'What mind is it that makes you see this circumstance as a difficulty?'

Ask an open-ended question in the peace of meditation.

Following this ask the question:

'What would this circumstance feel like if I were to think about it with a grateful mind?'

Explore this reflection; there is no set conclusion.

Just allow your mind to explore ... take your time.

If you feel your mind wandering, use your breathing to bring your awareness into the present moment and return to the reflection.

As your practice comes to a natural conclusion, determine to explore this reflection during the day.

...

We can simply ask ourselves at regular intervals throughout the day, and especially when we start to feel disturbed by something:

What would this circumstance feel like if it was filtered through a grateful mind?

Notes and Discussion

What are your current views concerning the origin of the problems in your life?

Does transforming your view increase the power in your mind?

Does changing your view bring more gratitude to your mind?

At the end of your day, write down five gratitudes.

Day 45

Challenges: Looking with wisdom

Virtually anyone involved in business will tell you at meetings that it is frowned upon to talk about 'problems'. We are encouraged instead to refer to them as 'challenges' or even as 'opportunities'. This approach requires a change of mind, and view. It is this theme that we are exploring in today's reflection; our potential to change our mental approach towards the circumstances that arise in our life.

If we have a trained and disciplined mind we can mentally approach any circumstance that occurs as an opportunity, a challenge for the growth and development of the positive mental attitude of gratitude.

With creative and positive thinking, we can start to bring gratitude into our experience and recognise that the challenge arising can encourage growth and development, appreciating that without it maybe this growth would not be possible. An understanding of this point and an ability to be able to hold this recognition in our daily life, is the mind of wisdom at work, and will enable us to generate gratitude for having the adversity.

We develop and nurture a way of thinking towards the circumstances that arise in our life that can give rise to peace and happiness. With this mental ability we will come to enjoy a stability of mind, where it doesn't waver. We empower ourselves to have one good day after another. How? Simply because we decide to have a good day. We no longer depend on our external circumstances to determine whether our day is going well or not. We have the confidence and knowledge to accomplish this.

Wisdom guides our mind so that we can think and reflect on circumstances in a way that directs us towards solutions. If we think about why anxiety arises in our life, it is because we dwell and reflect on 'what could go wrong' and the adverse conditions that could arise for us in the future.

For example:

What happens if work stops coming my way and I find myself with less money in the future?

What happens if this person decides to move out of my life and leave me on my own?

What if I enter this business venture and it is not materially successful?

What if this sore throat is an indication that I have a severe illness?

The anxiety arises as we are not reflecting on the potential adversity creatively. If we have confidence in our gratitude training we can be mentally secure, recognising that even if things don't work out in the way we wish, we can still keep a stable, positive mind, and possibly even enjoy the process. Following this way of thinking our gratitude training can start to naturally reduce our anxiety.

When things don't work out in our lives, and we have to experience unwished-for situations, we can learn to transform our view, see the circumstances as challenges, and encourage ourselves to develop gratitude at having the opportunity to train our mind.

Some cyclists love to climb hills; this can be a vigorous workout and test the cyclists' physical and mental strength; hills can help them to get into the flow state and let go of their stress. Some cyclists may even enjoy cycling uphill more than freewheeling downhill. For a non-cyclist, whose body is untrained, it may make no sense that they can enjoy climbing hills. But they may not ever have experienced the satisfaction of the view that awaits when they arrive at the top of a summit after having worked their way slowly up. Or how delicious food tastes and how well the body digests it after a day in the saddle, climbing mountains.

It's a viewpoint — the same with our training of the mind. Adversities are hills and mountains that we can climb with the right mental attitude. They can be opportunities to increase our mind of gratitude. Eventually, with a trained mind, the default response that we will come to have towards adversity is the mind of joyful gratitude.

Spend a few minutes bringing your attention into the present moment, direct your attention to your breathing, in a relaxed, calm manner.

Allow your thoughts from the past and the future to dissolve into the present moment.

Take an open look at your mind. Allow your thoughts to come and let them pass.

Reflect on your life and consider any challenging situations that you currently have to work with.

Gently ask yourself in the quiet of meditation:

Can I view this as a challenge?

What would this situation feel like if I were to approach it as an opportunity for growth?

Would it then be possible to develop gratitude?

Explore this reflection and allow your mind to naturally move towards gratitude.

Determine to take on the challenges of life with a resilient and grateful mind.

Hold this decision single-pointedly.

If you need some assistance with your meditation, you can engage in the following mindspace motivation.

As you breathe in say to yourself:
Breathing in, I allow my mind to become strong and stable.

As you breathe out say to yourself:
Breathing out, I determine to approach the challenges in my life with the positive mental attitude of gratitude.

When you are ready to bring your session to a close, determine to apply the mind of gratitude to the circumstances that arise in your life.

...

If we can understand and work with this reflection, we can start to appreciate and develop gratitude for whatever arises in our life, whether we wish for it or not. This approach doesn't mean to say we become an emotionless robot, far from it. We have the positive emotion of gratitude and peace, which allows us to enjoy every moment of our day.

Notes and Discussion

Consider some adversity that you currently have to experience in your life right now and consider how you could develop gratitude for it.

At the end of your day, write down five gratitudes.

Day 46

Patience: Enjoying the art of a peaceful mind

Just as a novice surfer will struggle and need persistence to train in catching the wave, so when we train in gratitude — especially grateful adversity — we need to apply effort, have a strong motivation and continuously renew our intention to practise. These essential factors will enable us to carry our training continuously. As a result of practising we will gain experience, confidence, and then consequently apply more effort. Training the mind is an art; as we become more skilled we can derive more enjoyment from each moment of the process.

Patience is an acceptance of any situation that arises. It is an engaged, positive, peaceful mind. It is a mind that doesn't allow us to sink into negativity and despondency as soon as a difficulty or challenge arises.

With proactive training in patience, we become mentally strong and primed for the challenges of human life. Our mind during our daily activities is balanced; it is not too tight and not too loose. With a daily patience practice we can make a seamless transition into the quiet space of formal meditation, with less distractions and disturbance in our mind. Just as the ocean is still, calm, and clear, deep beneath the waves, so, with patience in our mind, can our mental attitude be when the winds of change come and stir up our experience.

Just because someone in our life is feeling tense, stressed and unhappy, doesn't mean that we have to respond or feel the same way. Reacting in a defensive, agitated manner is a mental habit, the situation could be our opportunity to stay peaceful and calm. If we can learn to transform adversity with gratitude, we not only strengthen our own emotional health, we also help the person confronting us.

Patience doesn't mean that we always stay silent and don't respond, react or engage, or look to change the external situation.

It means, in this context, that we cultivate the ability to keep a peaceful mind at all times. It is quite a subtle experience and takes careful reflection to appreciate its meaning. It will help if we can train in the recommended meditation practices, to give us the strength of mind to integrate our understanding into our daily activities.

Please spend a few minutes bringing your attention into the present moment, directing your attention to your breathing in a relaxed, calm manner.

Allow thoughts of the past and the future to dissolve into the present moment.

Take an open look at your mind, let your thoughts and distractions pass as though they were clouds moving through the sky of your mind.

Please try to bring your attention inwards, observe your thoughts, invite them into your mind, but don't entertain them.

Let your mind become peaceful through looking gently at your thoughts.

Just abide in the present moment.

Reflect:

Through training my mind, I can keep a peaceful mind, regardless of the circumstances. All I need to do is keep gradually training my mind and increasing my wisdom through training in gratitude. If I can train my mind, mental stability will arise, and peace will come into my life.

Spend some quality time with this reflection, sitting with the experience and understanding for a short time.

Allow gratitude to arise for the opportunity that you now have to cultivate and develop this wisdom in your life, and for the many chances that are afforded to you to be able to train in the art of patience.

Calmly abide with this mind of gratitude.

When you are ready, conclude your practice with a determination to train proactively in patience throughout your life.

...

Far from patience making our mind weak and vulnerable, it will strengthen our resilience and bring a continuous source of positivity to our inner life, giving us the power to remain mentally stable whatever life throws at us.

In our training we can get to the point where we mentally thank those around us when they challenge us for providing the opportunity to practise patience. When a challenge arises, with a mind of gratitude, we can think:

This is now my opportunity to practise patience. With a patient mind, I can find resilience within and peace and happiness in my life.

Notes and Discussion

What circumstances in your life right now can help you train in the art of patience?

At the end of your day, write down five gratitudes.

Day 47

Sickness: Healing our body with gratitude

One of the main challenges that arise in our life can be when something unwished-for happens to our body. When our body is sick, this can function to bring down our mood and make us feel low and despondent. We can also spend valuable time right now worrying about potential illnesses that may come to our body in the future. When we are sick we must experience some form of physical suffering and pain; this doesn't automatically mean that we should feel low and unhappy. If this negative reaction arises, we add mental pain to our physical suffering.

With a trained mind, we can use sickness as our opportunity to develop patience and gratitude. With this wisdom our mind can become positive; with a positive mind our challenge becomes lighter, we are able to take the focus off ourself and our body, and consequently, we may recover from our sickness more speedily.

Our physical sickness can also reveal to us that it is time to take a break and rest from the busyness of life. Sickness is teaching us to stop and slow down. How kind of it! We can use our sickness as the opportunity to cultivate gratitude. Sickness is just sickness; whether it is a positive or negative experience depends on our attitude. Our body may be sick but, with a grateful attitude, we don't need to be.

The experience of sickness can also remind us of the people in the world right now who are experiencing suffering. With this way of thinking we can increase and develop our loving-kindness and compassion.

I remember speaking to my uncle when he was going through cancer treatment. He told me that for him the idea of the treatment when he was healthy was worse than when he was actually experiencing it. When he was undergoing the treatment he learned to accept the circumstances, and this eased the process. He found a creative flow where he started painting, and during this time of sickness, made many beautifully pictures. He managed to keep a calm mind during the process and in this way eased the adversity of the physical pain.

Gradually bring your attention into the present moment, focus gently on your breathing in a relaxed, calm manner.

Allow thoughts of the past and the future to dissolve into the present moment.

Observe your thoughts as they pass.

Bring to mind the times that you have been physically ill.

Consider when you will be physically ill in the future.

Reflect:

Whether this is something negative or positive depends on my mind and attitude, not the situation. With a trained mind, I can transform these circumstances and learn to develop patience, tolerance and compassion. In this way, physical sickness is teaching me; it is helping me to grow and develop. How fortunate I am to have these opportunities in my life! With this attitude, I can deal positively with the sickness that is arising.

Reflecting in this way, allow the mind of gratitude to grow.

Nourish the growth of gratitude in your mind. When it arises clearly, focus on it single-pointedly for as long as possible.

Calmly-abide with gratitude so that your entire mind mixes with this emotion. If you become distracted, use your breath to return your attention to the present moment and bring gratitude once again to mind.

You can stabilise your practice with the following mindful motivation:

As you breathe in, think to yourself:

Breathing in, I allow gratitude to stabilise my mind.

As you breathe out, think to yourself:

Breathing out, I let go of stress and confusion.

As your practice concludes, determine to carry your experience into the rest of your life, so you can learn to respond with gratitude naturally.

...

Notice the habitual responses and emotions you have when adversity arises; step back mentally, let them arise, feel the effects that they have on your body and mind, let them come, and then let them go. Allow the appreciation to arise for the fact that you can respond to circumstances in whichever way you choose to. You can remember the mindful motivation and try to repeat it if you feel busy and stressed.

...

When we busily multitask, and don't give ourselves time to pause, we create a perfect mental environment to become stressed and tired. This is why it is so important to allow ourselves to stop and reflect each day to regain our mental strength and clarity.

Notes and Discussion

Can you turn physical sickness into your gratitude teacher?

How do you think you can share this knowledge with loved ones and those close to you who are suffering from sickness?

At the end of your day, write down five gratitudes.

Day 48

Rudeness: Grounded in gratitude

Many of the mindful and gratitude reflections can seem possible when we are quietly reflecting upon them, but what about when we encounter others? Especially when we are on the receiving end of others' rudeness!

When we first put time and effort into our training of the mind, and become aware of our thoughts, we can start to notice others' lack of gratitude a little more acutely. It is essential to appreciate that when we train our mind the practices are firstly for us; they are to be taken personally not intellectually, and to be practised in a light-hearted manner.

What others choose to do with their minds is entirely up to them. If others are rude or impatient with us, if we are training in gratitude, this is another opportunity to practise. We can reflect that we are being offered the opportunity by this person to increase our patience and peace. Their behaviour is helping us to train our mind, if we wish, and we can begin to appreciate them for it. Without this person in our life at this time there would be no opportunity to practise patience.

It may almost seem slightly comical to develop gratitude in such a situation. Almost sarcastic, to think, 'Oh, I am so grateful for you being rude'. With enough strength and determination in our mind this attitude becomes possible for us to cultivate. We can become like a mental ninja.

Our natural human instinct, our natural response in challenging situations, is either fight or flight. With a trained mind we observe what is arising, let it pass, and our response is influenced by peace and patience. With training it becomes possible; we can progress and move forward.

Others' rudeness or attitude doesn't have to have a negative effect on us. If it does, we are the ones who must deal with the impact of this negative reaction within our body and mind, not them.

When our mind is trained, we can learn to enjoy the situations that arise in our life, regardless of others' attitudes or behaviour. In this way, we can learn to carry calm into and throughout our life, irrespective of what others are choosing to do or not do. This approach creates a stable experience of mental peace for us and those around us.

Of course, we have to be realistic and practise in accordance with our ability, situation, and circumstances. This teaching is not saying that we should physically tolerate everything that is happening to us. We must protect our physical and mental health.

This practice is specifically referring to how we mentally respond to situations. It is also not saying that we should suppress frustrated emotions. What it is offering is a chance to increase our resilience concerning the challenges that we face so that whatever happens to us, physically or verbally, we can mentally stay strong and protect ourself and others from increased suffering and stress.

Listen to the sounds around you mindfully, and gradually bring your attention into the present moment, directing your mind to your breathing in a relaxed, calm manner.

Breathe in positive energy, and breathe out frustration and stress.

Allow thoughts of the past and the future to dissolve into the present moment.

Take an open look at your mind, letting your thoughts and distractions pass.

Consider your life and the times you have become frustrated with others' rudeness and attitude.

Reflect:

Can these circumstances help me to train in patience and gratitude?

I can learn to deal with the experiences in my life with peace and see others as providing the opportunity to help me to accomplish this. How fortunate that I have the chance to train my mind and can learn to stay calm through the circumstances that arise in my day.

Reflecting like this, allow the mind of gratitude to arise, and try to hold it single-pointedly.

Try to calmly-abide from moment to moment with this mind. When the experience fades try not to follow distraction, instead bring the gratitude to mind and mix your attention with it.

As your session concludes, determine to hold gratitude in your mind throughout the day and night. Make the decision when you are with others not to entertain negativity.

...

This practice naturally leads to the next contemplation where, once again, as with the other practices presented in this text, we see others as our teachers who are guiding us to the mind of gratitude.

Notes and Discussion

Why do we get upset by rudeness; how can we turn this around?

Are others really kind if they are rude to us?

At the end of your day, write down five gratitudes.

Day 49

Hidden Teachers: Learning from our experience

In our final reflections on grateful adversity, we conclude by developing gratitude for our teachers. In previous meditations, we have contemplated the teachers in our life; those people who have obviously been in a position of learning, whom we go to and acquire knowledge from. In this contemplation, we are extending our appreciation to the teachers in our lives who help us to practise patience, tolerance, loving kindness, compassion, mindfulness and gratitude. With a creative approach, this can include everyone we will ever meet.

When we encounter those who appear to be the cause of our difficulties or problems we will most probably not see them as teachers, but as annoying people to be avoided.

To see someone as a teacher we must feel as though we have something to learn from the person, which requires an element of respect and a dose of humility within our mind.

With the wisdom that arises from the gratitude practices presented above, we start to cultivate an openness and appreciation towards all the people around us.

With training, we can learn to sidestep the knee-jerk, immediate, negative, emotional 'fight' response, which automatically arises to adversity, replacing it with a more creative, constructive attitude. All the reflections in this series on grateful adversity allow us to transform our view of others and put our mind in a position that will enable us to see them as our teachers.

We can recognise that someone who is rude, or shows us a bad attitude, can teach us about training in the art of patience. Or we can reflect on how the person who appears to be harming us, or is making our life difficult, is experiencing mental unrest and thereby develop compassion.

We are not looking down on the person and taking a 'holier than thou' approach; no, we look up to them as one of our teachers. That doesn't necessarily mean that we go along with them, or don't protect ourself and others. It merely means that our attitude, the mind that we have towards them, and the mind that we hold after the encounter, becomes positive.

This recognition provides us with a foundation for developing gratitude by reflecting that without the encounter, and having this person in our life, we would not have had the opportunity to grow and develop our mind. With this approach, we can make rapid progress with our training of the mind; we can grow and develop in all our encounters. Everywhere we go we can receive teachings.

With creativity this can also go beyond the scope of human beings. We can receive teachings from the weather, traffic lights, physical sickness; within any unwished-for situation there are opportunities to develop gratitude.

There was a great Indian meditation teacher called Atisha, who took a very practical version of Buddha's teachings from India to Tibet. When he travelled to Tibet from India he brought with him a cook. This cook was continually rude to him. There were many respectful Tibetans who asked him why he would always have this cook with him. He replied that for him this cook was very precious, and through spending time with him, he had the continuous opportunity to train in the art of patience. Although in India, Atisha had many famous Buddhist teachers, for him, this cook was his greatest teacher as, due to the presence of him in his life, he was able to practise patience.

It is said, in their advanced training, those with great skill in the practices of training the mind, from the Tibetan tradition of meditation known as 'Lojong', would make reverent prayers to encounter challenges and difficulties so they could train their mind and have endless opportunities to grow!

Please bring your attention to the present moment, direct your attention to your breathing in a relaxed, calm manner.

Allow thoughts of the past and the future to naturally dissolve.

As you breathe in, allow your posture to straighten, and as you breathe out, let your shoulders drop and body to relax.

Take an open look at your thoughts; let them pass through your mind like waves arising out of the ocean.

Reflect on all the opportunities that you have in your life for teachings, whether it is from people or the situations that arise.

Reflect:

How fortunate I am to have all these opportunities to encourage me to train my mind. With a creative, wise approach, I have many chances each day for growth and development.

Reflect in this way until the mind of gratitude arises for the opportunities for teachings that you have. Try to hold it with single-pointed concentration for as long as possible.

When gratitude fades, try to renew the contemplation until the mind arises again and hold it once more. In this way, you start to deepen your experience of gratitude.

Try to calmly abide with this mind of gratitude for as long as you can.

As your practice ends, make the intention to carry your grateful intention into your daily life.

If you like, you could make your reflection specific to one person, and encourage yourself to learn from that relationship. In this way, you can prime your mind for all the teachings that are going to present themselves to you.

Towards the end of your session, dedicate all the good energy from your meditation, so that you can increase your practice and make positive progress with your training in gratitude.

...

This attitude will transform our life. Our habits are deep and can lead us to respond to challenging situations in a habitual way, however, this doesn't mean that when we recall a difficult circumstance we have to retain the thread of negativity. We can reflect that we have been given the opportunity to cultivate gratitude, and encourage ourself to transform our recollection into a positive one.

Just as farmers use manure to increase the growth of their crops, so can we use the toxicity that arises as part of our human existence to strengthen the development and growth of gratitude within our mind. With the right mental attitude and confidence in the instructions, adversity can propel us quickly toward a happy, contented life.

Notes and Discussion

How many teachers do you currently have in your life?

What ways can you remember this practice in your daily activities?

Can you develop gratitude while at the same time removing yourself from a challenging situation?

Do you think gratitude is always appropriate to generate?

At the end of your day, write down five gratitudes.

Grateful Future

Confident decisions

Day 50

Ocean: Reflecting on the vastness

In today's practice we take stock and reflect upon the great profundity of the practice of gratitude.

As we have discovered through investigating this precious attitude over the previous seven chapters, there are many levels of training and a myriad of different routes into this mind.

When we start to train in gratitude we are able to appreciate how it can become the perfect marriage with our mindfulness practice. As our training deepens we develop the ability to be more in the present moment, finding ourselves less prone to multi-tasking and being pre-occupied with the future and past. This book and mental training offers encouragement, allowing you to establish and develop this mind daily. Naturally, as this mindful habit grows, our gratitude will only need a little nudge forward to arise almost effortlessly.

Mindful training leads seamlessly into gratitude. If we walk down the street mindfully, as our attention focuses, we can see deeper into our reality. We can go beneath the surface and appreciate the history of kindness. We can consider all those who have worked in the past to create this amenity. This insight into the network of human kindness, which allows gratitude to arise in our mind, can only be discovered through our mindful awareness.

When I was considering this chapter earlier, I took a walk through a local park and noticed someone mowing the lawn and tending to the ground. As a result of this activity, I was able to enjoy my time in the park. As I was mindfully walking through the park, I was able to notice this with a positive mind, cultivate an appreciation and gratitude for the work that I was on the direct receiving end of and, if I wanted to go further, all the previous work that had taken place in the park over the weeks, months, and years.

Although mindful training encourages us to be in the moment, within the present, there can be an appreciation for the past and a hope for the future.

Gratitude training, combined with our mindful practice, helps us to become aware of where we are and provides a more in-depth insight into our everyday experience.

It is in the everyday where our gratitude and mindfulness training comes alive. To initiate our practice we can read books, attend retreats and workshops, but the authentic experience of our training will come through our remembrance and integration of the instructions we have received into our everyday life.

Offering new attention to what appears 'routine and mundane' makes it no longer routine and mundane. Looking with new eyes at the ordinary helps it appear extraordinary, just as a young child is mesmerised by the world and the experiences they have, enjoying a mind that is continually refreshing itself. With mindful gratitude we can see our world as both fresh and engaging.

Just today, when I was making my way to the train station, I saw a grandmother taking her grandchild for a walk in the pushchair. She had stopped at a bridge that was overlooking a dual carriageway. It appeared, with an ordinary perspective, there was nothing special to see. The child, however, was captivated by the moving traffic. The child was entirely in the moment watching the flow. Perhaps we have seen moving traffic hundreds of times so, for us, it may not be eye-catching, not worth stopping for due to the many jobs and grand plans ahead of us. With this rushing attitude, we can miss what is right in front of us, what is right under our nose.

When we start training in gratitude it's like we have discovered a water source within. We firstly connect with the very slight dripping tap within us, appreciating that we have this mind, and with the right training we can encourage its growth. As we progress with our practice, we can start to see that this gratitude can grow continually.

Buddha himself pointed out that even a tap dripping will eventually fill a bucket. So we can appreciate that this training develops over time. There is much more gratitude within us than just to fill a bucket; there is an endless source of this positive energy. If we can take the time to train our mind, the flow of our gratitude can develop from an occasional dripping tap, to a full flow of water, to a babbling brook, to a steady stream, to a broad river, and finally to a vast ocean.

With this practice, we reflect on the extent and potential that we have for the growth of this attitude within our consciousness and consider the amount of gratitude that can arise in the future, which can nourish and sustain us. Once again, we cultivate and meditate on gratitude for having this extraordinary experience.

With the ocean meditation practice, we take the time to reflect on the vastness of this incredible practice of gratitude.

Please bring your attention to the sensation of your breathing, gathering your mind into the present moment away from distracting thoughts.

Gently turn your attention inwards:

Reflect on the vastness of this gratitude training and how you can gradually increase it until it becomes limitless. Recognise the incredible potential for gratitude within your mind.

Sit with the recognition of the potential for gratitude within your mind.

With the recognition of this ocean-like gratitude that you can develop, bathe your mind in the appreciation for having this time in your life to awaken this emotion.

Knowing deeply your potential, develop gratitude.

Allow an ocean of gratitude to arise, while you simultaneously bathe your mind in the vastness of your potential to develop this mind.

If you recognise something is of value you will make sure that you don't waste it; with this understanding allow yourself to be guided by the mind of gratitude to make the intention not to waste this precious opportunity.

Depending on your mind and how distracted it may be, you may have to repeat this contemplation many times to bring it alive.

Remember throughout your meditation that if your mind becomes distracted, use the sensation of your breath and mindful awareness of your body, to bring your attention to the moment. With your mind refocused, continue with your contemplation and gratitude training.

If you need assistance with the meditation and help to retain focus, try the following mindspace motivation.

As you breathe in mentally say, *breathing in, I allow an ocean of gratitude to arise in my heart.*

As you breathe out mentally say, *breathing out, I wish for others to experience an ocean of gratitude in their lives.*

When you are ready to bring your session to a close, determine to integrate your experience of gratitude into your daily life, and to take all the opportunities that are presented to you to generate this ocean-like mind.

Conclude your training with the intention to increase your gratitude practice on behalf of everyone in your life, society, community and world.

Notes and Discussion

How does recognising your ocean-like potential help to uplift your mind?

How does a positive attitude improve your relationships?

At the end of your day, write down five gratitudes.

Day 51

Deep: Penetrating the depths of our mind

In our busy, modern, materialistic world, it is rare to spend time sitting and quietly reflecting, and even when we do our mind can be full of distractions and busyness. We may feel unable to stop thinking about all the jobs and tasks that we need to do, while contending with all our experiences from the past impressed within our mind.

However, if we try to make time each day to remember gratitude, are patient with our training, attend occasional retreats, and are not in a rush to see results, we will gain experience of the world beneath the stress. We will start to appreciate the vast depths and profundity of the human mind, in particular our own mind!

As we explored in the previous practice, our mind is as vast as the ocean. For much of the time, we are on the surface of our mind, being tossed and turned by our distractions and worries. When we train consistently in mindful meditation, we are starting to awaken the peace that resides within. As we begin to gain experience, we can discover and enjoy an authentic calm and happiness, which is rare to witness in todays busy world.

Our mind's essential nature is boundless and unobstructed. It is our conceptual thoughts and, in particular, our doubt and negativity, which restricts our growth. Once we have gained an insight into the potential of our ocean-like mind we can be filled with energy and enthusiasm, to keep journeying and discovering the world within.

If we have managed to enjoy a small amount of calm and peace from our practice, a reduction of stress, and an increase in happiness in our everyday life, this is an indication that more is possible. If we keep practising, we grow organically from where we are. It is unnecessary to compare ourselves to those around us or require validation for our practice; we appreciate our experience and encourage ourself that there is more to come if we keep training our mind. In the same way, a clematis budding and revealing a small flower indicates its potential for growth into a glorious bloom. If nourished and given the right conditions and care, this clematis can transform into a full blossoming flower that can grow and flourish year after year. Likewise, the small signs in our practice are an indication of the depths and potential that exists within us.

In today's meditation we take the opportunity to step back from the busyness, to experience the depths of our mind, while developing gratitude for having the chance at this point in our life to enjoy this.

As our mind and body begin to relax into the meditation space, we can establish a daily habit, our training will start to feel natural, and we can start to enjoy a first-hand experience.

Please bring your attention to the present moment and ease your mind into the natural sensation of the breath.

Spend a short time observing its flow, and the effect that it has as it travels around your body.

Notice the cooling sensation as you breathe in, and the warm sensation as you breathe out, at the tip of your nostrils.

Allow your mind to let go of distractions and absorb completely into the journey of your breath.

As the distractions in your mind begin to pacify, start to direct your attention towards the flow of your thoughts as they arise and dissolve.

Observe them as they pass through your mind.

Follow their flow.

Gently look deeper into your thoughts and allow your mind to relax.

Watch your mind and recognise the vast potential for gratitude that you have within you.

Try to see beyond the thoughts that pass and go deeper into the nature of your mind, which is peaceful and calm.

You don't need to fabricate this experience as it will naturally arise of its own accord if you are patient in the space of meditation.

As your session progresses, allow the mind of gratitude to arise for having a human mind and being able to access its extraordinary potential.

Calmly-abide in this space for as long as you can.

As your practice draws to a close, determine to carry your experience into everyday life, so that your actions of body, speech and mind are influenced by gratitude.

...

Notes and Discussion

How can you make more time in your day to spend in meditation?

Would you consider going on a meditation retreat, and how long?

At the end of your day, write down five gratitudes.

Day 52

Confidence: Moving forward with appreciation

There are many different types of confidence that we can benefit from. When we train in mindful meditation, there is a specific type of quiet, calm confidence that will arise as a result of the inner strengthening of our mental training, as our mind becomes progressively more positive and focused.

Gratitude is a naturally virtuous and upbeat mind. With this attitude, we start to have a more positive relationship with ourself, our past, our present, and our future. Due to this, the relationships we have with others improve, as the way we relate to others and our perspective of them is a natural reflection of how we relate to ourself.

As the days go by, and we progress with our training, we allow gratitude to start to influence our actions of body, speech, and mind. In this way we move forward, away from past negativities. We can be happy in the present moment, letting go of the past and embracing our future with appreciation. Due to being influenced by gratitude, we can take this perspective into our future. We can learn to be open and appreciative of the daily experiences that we have on a moment by moment basis.

Today's mindfulness practice is an uplifting nod of gratitude to the experiences that await us in the future. We can be sure from our gratitude contemplations that what awaits us in the future will depend on the kindness of others. We move forward with a positive, quiet confidence in our ability to generate gratitude and encourage ourself to grow. With this attitude and state of mind, we will naturally draw positive experiences to us.

Take your time to settle into the present moment, and gently bring your attention into your body.

Notice the sensation that arises in your body and its contact with the ground.

Press down gently on the floor beneath you and allow your posture to straighten.

As you breathe in, come to the present moment and, as you breathe out, let go of the stress in your body and mind.

Allow your mind to settle and gradually absorb into the present moment, by observing the sensation of your breathing.

Bring your mind to the experience of gratitude.

Remember and recognise the kindness that you receive from others. All the small things, everything that has arisen in your life, have come from others.

Encourage gratitude to arise. Focus completely on this mind.

Calmly-abide from moment to moment with this state.

Consider your future experience and recognise how everything that will come to you will depend on others.

Let gratitude manifest.

With gratitude in your mind, allow a strong determination and confident, positive energy to arise. Cultivate a decision to move forward in your life with gratitude and appreciation.

Hold this uplifting determination for as long as possible, and intend to carry this mind into the future.

Notes and Discussion

How do you think the type of confidence we are generating here differs from others?

What relationship does gratitude have with confidence?

At the end of your day, write down five gratitudes.

Day 53

Positivity: Reflecting on the strength of gratitude

In this reflection we contemplate the gratitude that we have generated thus far on the course, and recognising the incredible, positive power of this training. Meditating on gratitude brings an abundance of positivity into our mind and leads to happy results in our life.

When our mind is positive it becomes stable, enabling us to deal with challenges and difficulties in a creative, selfless way and move forward. Just as a seasoned surfer has transformed their perception of waves, and has subsequently learned to enjoy them, so we can come to transform the difficulties of our human life.

We reflect on gratitude and allow our mind to uplift and become full of positive energy. There is no limit to how much positivity we can grow in our mind. We have limitless potential. Why? Within our mind there is no boundary; the only boundaries are our limited conceptual thoughts.

We conclude our meditation intending to carry our positive mind into the rest of our day, making the intention, 'today I am going to keep a positive, grateful mind for everyone'.

Please bring your attention to the present moment.

Use the focus on your breathing to guide your attention into your body, and start to abide single-pointedly with this experience.

Give yourself space and time to reflect on the gratitude that you have developed during the course, and the positivity that has arisen as a consequence of cultivating this mind.

With a light, joyful mind reflect on gratitude, using whichever contemplation has worked for you; you could use the grateful mantra to encourage this attitude to grow within.

As you breathe in, gently say to yourself: *I am so fortunate.*

As you breathe out, gently say to yourself: *Others are so kind.*

Combine your breathing with this mantra, say these words gently to yourself to allow your focus and concentration to improve.

Consider the positivity that comes into your mind when gratitude is present, enjoy this reflection, and allow your mind to fill with positive energy. Abide within this state for a short time.

Bring gratitude to the forefront of your mind and mix your attention with it. Allow your mind to mix with this positive state as though you were pouring water into water.

When you choose to conclude your session, make the intention to carry gratitude into the rest of your day and life.

...

If you can integrate gratitude training into your daily life, then you will start to see great results arising.

Notes and Discussion

What difference does it make to a situation if you can reflect on it with a positive mental attitude?

How can you use the mind of gratitude to help you when your mind is under the influence of negativity?

At the end of your day, write down five gratitudes.

Day 54

Decision: Moving towards a grateful conclusion

In this session, we are going to explore the power of decision making and, in particular, constructing the decision to train in gratitude now and in the future.

One of my teachers from the Buddhist Centre where I lived used to say regularly, "When people say that they don't have time to meditate, what they are really saying is that their intention is not strong enough, or that their decision is not clear."

If we wish to succeed in anything, we need to focus and have a strong decision to carry out that action. We are reading this text because we decided to read it and, if we manage to stay focused and reflect on it, this is as a result of having made a decision to do so.

If we are interested in strengthening and focusing on our training in gratitude, both now and in the future, we need to strengthen our decision to practise. The stronger our decision to train in gratitude the more we will find ourself practising, and remembering to integrate this attitude in our life.

When days go by, and we are not practising, this is simply because our decision has faded. However busy we may be, we can always cultivate gratitude in the back of our mind. To help make this a reality, as mentioned previously, it can be extremely helpful to spend time at the beginning of the day setting our intention.

If we can work on strengthening and establishing our decision, our ability and the time that we have to practise will be abundant. How do we work on our decision to train in gratitude? We focus on the benefits of the practice. There are an abundant amount of benefits that will arise from training in gratitude, and we have explored this throughout the course; let us now familiarise ourself again with the main benefits that will come into our life from engaging in this positive training:

Our mind is naturally uplifted.

We increase the positivity, and thereby the happiness in our mind.

We strengthen the direct antidote to the mind of depression.

The relationship that we have with ourself improves, as our mind is clearer, more positive and encouraging.

The relationships that we have with others, now, in the past and in the future, improve.

We naturally feel more connected and integrated with the world around us.

Our mindful practice is strengthened, flavoured, and energised, with this positive state of mind.

Let us now meditate on these benefits, bringing into our contemplations our experience and observation of the direct benefits that we have enjoyed as a result of following this course. Reflecting on these benefits brings us to an intention to train continuously in this mind. Consequently, we will have the energy to train and thereby be able to enjoy the fruits of this practise continually in the future.

There is a growing body of scientific research revealing the benefits of mindfulness, gratitude and compassion training; for me, the best research that we can rely on as individuals, regarding the benefits of this training, comes from our own experience.

This intention will start to become our greatest asset and will open the door to experiencing all the great benefits of this training in the future.

Please begin your practice by bringing your attention to your body and gathering your mind inside.

Notice the sensation of your body against the floor, and press slightly down against it, allowing this process to connect you with the present moment.

Allow your back to straighten and your shoulders to relax.

Focus on your breathing, stay gently with the inhalation and exhalation.

Notice all the sensations as your breath enters and leaves your body.

Stay with your breathing for a short time, until your mind starts to settle.

With a calm mind reflect on the great benefits of gratitude practice:

Gratitude will uplift my mind.

It is the foundation for all positive states of mind.

Gratitude will improve the relationship and conversation that I have with myself.

Gratitude will function to enhance the connection that I have with others.

Gratitude will bring calm and peace into my life.

Gratitude acts as protection from depressed ways of viewing the world around me.

Contemplate these great benefits, along with any more that you may have from your first-hand experience of training your mind.

Gradually allow the intention to train in gratitude to arise.

When this intention arises, try to hold it single-pointedly and abide with it for as long as possible.

If your decision fades, or your mind becomes distracted, return to contemplating the benefits of gratitude until the decision arises again.

Stay with this decision for as long as possible.

When you are ready to bring your meditation session to an end, make the intention to carry gratitude into your life, to practise both now and in the future.

In the break between this and the next session keep reflecting on the benefits of the practice of gratitude, and strengthen your mind.

...

I can't underestimate the importance of building our intention to practise. With a strong decision, we can overcome all obstacles and our gratitude practice can grow and evolve each day.

The great Indian Buddhist master, Shantideva, gave encouraging advice regarding what to say to ourself when we feel discouraged, lazy, lacking in motivation, distracted and losing ourselves in worldly enjoyments:

'I shall conqueror all obstacles, and none shall conquer me.'

This intention helps us to keep a positive, confident mind that will propel us forward in our training. Keep making this positive decision and allow it to influence your thoughts and actions.

I often say in the live classes that I teach that our future happiness doesn't need to be a lottery; we can secure our future happiness by approaching our gratitude training systematically, with an organised mind. Step by step we can establish all the conditions for a happy mind. We can make progress with our inner training of gratitude, if we approach it in a professional manner.

When you see someone achieving worldly success they approach their work with focus and determination, applying consistent effort and not expecting to obtain or achieve results automatically, just because they want them. They will work out what they need to do to achieve success, determine to do this, visualise the success and apply themselves accordingly to making this happen. We need to follow the same approach with our inner training of the mind.

Notes and Discussion

What are the main benefits of gratitude training that you have experienced?

How can you carry your gratitude further into your daily existence?

At the end of your day, write down five gratitudes.

Day 55

Power: Building grateful power within our mind

As we train in the mind of gratitude and keep strengthening our decision to practise, we start to build the power in our mind. With each meditation the strength builds. Meditation practice helps to train the mind. In the same way that we develop our body when we train in the gym, so it is when we engage in mind training exercises, we build the strength within.

To overcome negativity in our mind, we need inner strength to overpower it. Our mind follows whatever it is familiar with; the more we train the more familiar we become. As we become familiar with this positive, virtuous state of mind, inner strength arises, and negativity has less chance to take a foothold; if it does there is less inclination and tendency to entertain it.

Although gratitude is a very peaceful, gentle mind, it provides us with the inner strength to conquer negativity. Negative states of mind have less chance to grow and evolve within our consciousness, as gratitude develops. In this meditation we develop gratitude and enjoy the experience of the power that this mind provides us with to overcome our negativity.

Bring your attention to the present moment.

Listen gently to the sounds around you. Allow your mind to gather inwards. Listen to the breath inside you.

Start to notice the rising and falling of your body. If your mind is distracted, place your hands on your navel to feel the rising and falling of your body in time with your breathing.

Allow your mind to rest, becoming present, gentle and peaceful, as you become one with the breathing.

Let any thoughts about the past and future pass through your mind, and allow yourself to relax, let go and move on.

Reflect on the experience of gratitude that you have had during the course.

Recognise the positive energy that this attitude can bring to your mind and life.

Connect with this power within your mind. Appreciate the growth of this power and how it can transform your mental state.

Allow your mind to become filled with gratitude, and let yourself appreciate in the quiet of meditation that you can build this experience.

Take the time to appreciate that there is no limit for this growth.

Fully mix your attention with this virtuous mind of gratitude.

If your mind becomes distracted, use the sensation of the breath to bring your attention into the present moment.

Calmly-abide with gratitude, and enjoy the positive power that it brings to you.

Stay with gratitude for as long as you can.

As the practice comes to its natural conclusion, make the intention to use the power of gratitude in your daily life.

Try to carry the mind of gratitude into the rest of your day.

Make the intention to use your interactions with the world to strengthen your mind.

...

Notes and Discussion

How do you feel that gratitude empowers your mind?

If you allow yourself to be influenced by gratitude, what do you think will happen to your inner life?

At the end of your day, write down five gratitudes.

Day 56

Beginning: Carrying gratitude full circle

This reflection has so much depth we could spend a whole book exploring it. In the future, there will be this opportunity. For now, we will just touch on this theme and take our gratitude practise to a deeper level.

With gratitude in our mind, we reflect on the benefits that we receive throughout our life; we reflect on the positives in all our experiences. These benefits may initially appear but, for the duration of our training and a deeper practise, we need some further encouragement to add power to our intention.

In Chapter Seven, on grateful adversity, we explored developing gratitude towards adverse situations. Challenges arise as life progresses. Generally no inner training is offered by our elders or teachers in how to deal with them. We have to decide on the spot how we react and respond, and gradually learn from our experiences. Our reaction can be something that we imitate from our parents, habituated behaviour that we have slipped into, or we have a deeper, more spontaneous, protective response based on our survival instincts.

If we start to allow our experience of life to be influenced by gratitude, we will have more familiarity with responding to circumstances with this uplifting attitude.

Ageing, sickness and death are the three main challenges that we have to eventually face in our life. On this last day, let us take our practise a little deeper and consider that, if we are grateful for our life, we will naturally, eventually, be grateful for our death. Death is the natural conclusion of our life; everything that is born must eventually pass. We see death around us, all the time. We see impermanence at play continuously.

We are only able to have all the experiences that arise in our life if we eventually die; the richness of our entire life stems from it being impermanent. Our human life arises solely from us being born. We must appreciate that everything that is born must eventually cease.

Reflecting sincerely on our impermanence, we can begin to have gratitude for our death; we can use the time in our life as a way to reflect on all the good fortune that we have experienced within our life and the kindness that we have received from others.

We can appreciate, when we bring the realisation of impermanence into our mind, that every moment of our life is precious and develop gratitude. If we step back from the busyness of our life, we can see that it is a miracle to be alive, to stay alive and to be able to enjoy each day. Every moment is precious. The moments that we have left in our lives are finite; they will eventually come to an end. This understanding of impermanence, mixed with gratitude, allows us to make the most of the time that we have left, and we feel encouraged not to waste these precious moments.

One of my students passed away when he was thirty-six. I went to see him in a hospice just before he died. He was a practitioner of meditation. The experience of suddenly being diagnosed with cancer transformed his mind. His practise became very strong. When I went to see him on his deathbed, he spoke to me and shared his thoughts about the kindness of the staff who were looking after him and those relatives who had made an effort to come and see him. His mind was strong, and his attitude was incredibly positive. How was this possible? He had trained his mind before, while also having a strong intention to carry the experience of gratitude with him through his life.

He approached his death with great lightness, grace, respect and openness; dying with the influence of gratitude in his mind also assured and inspired all those around him. He was able to bring gratitude into his mind at the most challenging moment of his life, because he had trained previously. There is no reason why we can't carry this gratitude intention that we are training in here to the time of our death.

It is helpful for us to appreciate that all the work we put into the training of our mind right now will benefit our future self. The more positivity we encourage to grow in our mind the more we will derive enjoyment and benefit from our training in the future.

From this story, we can see in even the most challenging moments of our life that, with a trained mind, we can bring gratitude to play, and allow our mind to be strong and uplifted. Reflecting on our impermanence every day (ideally) is far from morbid and depressing. It empowers and strengthens our mind, like adding an engine to our practice, encouraging us to focus on what is important and meaningful. Let us now meditate on this theme.

Please bring your attention to the present moment.

Gradually bring your focus to the sensation of the breathing.

Focus on the natural inhalation and exhalation; try to follow the complete journey around your body.

As you breathe in, allow yourself to arrive in the present moment.

As you breathe out, try to let go of stress and distraction.

Bring to mind gratitude for the life that you have.

Start to acknowledge how your breath is so precious and also fragile.

Generate gratitude for your life and your breath.

Reflect how, one day, this process will stop.

Try to allow the knowledge to dawn within your mind that your life will one day come to a completion.

Sit with this for a short time, while not forgetting the mind of gratitude.

Allow this understanding and appreciation to bring forth in your mind the strong intention not to waste a moment of your life, but to use it wisely to train your mind and be of benefit to others; to seize every moment.

Focus on this determination for as long as possible.

If your mind becomes distracted, use your breath to bring your attention to the present moment.

You can also use the following mindspace motivation to bring your attention inwards:

Breathing in, I understand the impermanence of my life.

Breathing out, I determine not to waste a single moment.

When you are ready to bring your session to a conclusion, make the decision to carry this awareness of impermanence into your life and not to waste a single moment.

...

The breath is all that keeps us alive. One day this process will stop. Our life is impermanent; due to this we can enjoy all the beauty of human life. One day we will breathe out and not breathe in again. It's as simple as that. The world will carry on just fine.

Gratitude is a positive mental attitude and acts as an antidote to negative states of mind. Our life is short. With the impermanence reflection we can appreciate this and are encouraged to use our moments, minutes, hours, days, weeks, months and years, wisely.

We are motivated to shine the light of our precious attention on the goodness in our lives and allow ourselves to be thoroughly influenced by the mind of gratitude, recognising that we can be influenced and healed by this mind throughout our life.

We can reflect and review our entire life with gratitude, starting from the time we were carried in our mother's womb through to our final breath. In between, we begin by developing an appreciation for the obvious kindness that we were on the receiving end of. As our training grows and develops, we can start to shine our gratitude on more challenges, circumstances, situations and people. With a growing resilience we can have the courage and confidence to develop gratitude for the adversities.

What is success? What is failure? With respect to success and failure in our life, there is no need to mentally adhere to a definitive rule that is made externally based on the convention of our society. We can decide for ourselves. Concerning our training in gratitude, we can say that we are successful in our life if we can use the circumstances that arise to empower us to be able to develop a grateful mind.

Gratitude can give us the confidence and courage to move forward, believe in ourself, our hopes and dreams, and be empowered to progress along the mindful path.

Notes and Discussion

What is your understanding of success and failure?

What pressure do you put on yourself to succeed? Is this helpful?

Can you think about death in a positive way? What are your thoughts?

At the end of your day, write down five gratitudes.

CONCLUSION

This text offers a series of fifty-six practices, covering eight main themes. There could quite easily have been a year of gratitude, but we start, however, with eight weeks. I feel this period allows us to gain an insight into a theme and sufficient time to decide how to integrate the content.

During the process of writing this text, it was a challenge to decide which gratitude practices to omit. What I encourage you to do, upon completion of this text, is to become creative with your practice; design your own original gratitude practices. As mentioned several times during the book, gratitude is a natural expression of our mindful training. If we are fully present with our actions, we naturally start to appreciate the moments and see beyond the surface, beyond the object.

The first step of mindful training is to see and witness, first-hand, the present; engaging fully with each moment.

For example, if we are taking a shower, the first step is noticing the shower, using our senses to be fully aware as we take a shower. How many times have we taken a shower and not been in the present moment, but somewhere in the future or past?

If we are mindful when we take a shower, we will be in the present, shining the light of our attention on each moment, being aware of the water and the sensations in our body, our breathing, and the thoughts passing through our mind. This awareness leads to a mind of appreciation for simply being able to take a shower and having access to clean water. We can then see our network, the kindness chain we are connected with and develop gratitude for all those who work to provide the facilities for us to enjoy. Gratitude arises because we are mindful and will continue to arise naturally throughout our life, if we can maintain our awareness in the present moment.

Our increased attention and interest in the present moment will open the door to a grateful world. We can take any activity that we engage in and mix our mind of gratitude with it. For example: grateful sleep, grateful walking, grateful talking, grateful gazing, grateful listening, grateful driving. If we can emphasise mindful training our gratitude comes alive, and we can create gratitude practices wherever we go.

We start this training by exploring how to **meditate** on gratitude. Taking our time to slow down and step back from the busyness of life. Appreciating that if we learn to meditate correctly, we can create the space in our mind to reflect, contemplate and gain a more profound experience of this precious mind.

We then gain insight into the **grateful to-go** practices, which empower us to carry our grateful practices into everyday life. We feel inspired that we can continue with this training as we are going about our daily activities, thus discovering a powerful way to continually uplift our mind.

To help us concentrate, we spend time focusing on the sensation of our **breath**, and combine our gratitude with this process, so that we can stabilise our ability to stay in the present moment, thereby taking our grateful practice to a deeper level.

Turning our attention inwards, we recognise the **seeds** and potential that reside in our heart for having a deep, stable experience, using this understanding as a basis for cultivating a positive identity.

As this training comes alive, when we integrate it into our daily life, we explore the activities that we continually engage in; one of them being **eating**. We take our training to the dining table and mix gratitude with the moments that we eat and drink.

Naturally following on from this chapter we work with the concept of how we can carry gratitude into our **relationships**, thereby stabilising our interaction with others, and providing ourself with a positive filter that we can use when we communicate with our friends, family, and all the people we meet as we move through our life.

As we progress and work through the training a question will arise: how can I develop gratitude towards a person or situation when I feel that I haven't benefitted from them? In the **adversity** chapter, we address this question and explore how to bring gratitude to the challenges that arise in our life. We take our practice deeper so that we can transform adverse conditions into our grateful path.

Finally, we look to the **future** and cultivate the intention to carry our training into the rest of our life. We appreciate that we can invest in our future mental health. We secure happiness for our future self by familiarising our mind with gratitude and intending to practice in the future. We think of our future and consider putting money aside for this time, but how often do we consider putting minds aside; how often do we consider positive mental investment? We take a mental investment perspective for our future in the final chapter.

Throughout the text, we have been watering the seeds within our mind for the cultivation and growth of the virtuous mind of gratitude. Gratitude is not something new. We already have this precious mind and express it regularly; now having completed this course we have the methods to gently grow gratitude in our heart, so we are nourished and positively guided by its presence.

I am grateful that you have taken the time to work through and engage with these practices. I have experienced for myself some of the benefits of having been influenced by this mind and seen the positive effect that training in these meditations has on students who have attended my live classes. I hope that you can also come to experience first-hand all the great benefits of training in gratitude.

CONDENSED VERSION

*If you are short of time and wish to go
straight to the practices, try reflecting
on the verses below*

GRATEFUL MEDITATIONS

Designing our future

With a creative intention

Settling in the moment

With calm

Connecting with our nature

Abiding

Moving forward

...

GRATEFUL-TO-GO

—

Rising with a smile, we appreciate

Water

The roof over our head

Our transportation

The services we receive

The health in our body

The network of kindness

...

GRATEFUL BREATHS

___

Abiding

We protect our mind

Remembering the kindness

A miracle breath

Taking our time

Drop by drop

Awakening to each moment

...

GRATEFUL SEEDS

———

Settling into the now

We find calm

As the waves break

We dive into our potential

With appreciation

We identify with the peace

Growing in our mind

...

GRATEFUL EATING

Recognising the kind-chain

We take a grateful breakfast

And a mindful coffee

Preparing with care

We enjoy a lunch break

And a slow supper

With harmony and peace

...

GRATEFUL RELATIONSHIPS

———

Appreciating our past

Opening our eyes to the future

Finding peace with those closest

We dive into our history

With gratitude to those who sustain us

Looking deeper

We open to kindness

...

GRATEFUL ADVERSITY

___

A positive perspective

Transforming our view

Looking with wisdom

Enjoying a peaceful mind

Healing our body with gratitude

We are grounded

Learning from experience

...

GRATEFUL FUTURE

———

Reflecting on the vastness

We penetrate the depths

Moving forward

With the strength of gratitude

Directing a grateful conclusion

We build power within the mind

Carrying gratitude full circle

...

NEXT STEPS

Deepen your experience on the Mindspace+ programme

Guide to the Mindful Way of Life: The beginners guide

Mindspace+: Build the foundation for a deeper practice

Loving Kindness: Practices to enhance communication

Improving Concentration: Meditations to help improve focus

Zen Mindfulness: Minimising clutter and becoming present

Wisdom: Developing insight and inner peace

Guide to the Positive Way of Life: A positive guide

Patience: Learning how to keep a calm and stable mind

Fearless: Reducing obstacles, increasing confidence

Compassion: Meditations to nourish our incredible potential

Happy: How to keep a happy, positive mind

Freedom: Leaving behind negativity, enjoying mental freedom

Inner Strength: Increasing mental resilience

For more details, please visit:
www.mindspace.org.uk/mindspace-online

ACKNOWLEDGMENTS

This book was written over a period of three years. I started writing the content when I was travelling through Japan during the winter of 2016. My time there provided a perfect opportunity to reflect and meditate on gratitude. To be on the receiving end of such wonderful public service each day was humbling. I thank all the people whom I encountered on this trip who inspired me to write this book.

Upon returning, I delivered a Mindspace+ course entitled Gratitude. I introduced this theme to small groups of students across the West Midlands, over an eight week course. Each day I would send students a short email with an essential practice to engage in. The feedback was positive. As the days went by, I felt the beneficial effects on my own mind, from teaching and reflecting on these instructions. I decided it would be worthwhile to write a book that covered the essential themes of the Gratitude course. So I thank this first group of students who came to these classes in the winter of 2017.

The practice of gratitude is like saying 'thank you' continually to the world around us. When I step back and reflect on the people who have helped manifest this book, the network is countless.

I thank you, the reader, for taking the time to reflect on these words, and making it worthwhile for me to have spent time writing this book.

Gratitude leads us along the compassionate path, to work continually for others with a joyful, happy heart, with the intention to repay the infinite kindness that we continually received. Writing this book is an expression of my wish to give something back to the world from which I have received so much.

Notes

shukran | ngiyabonga | dankie | faleminderit | Շնորհակալություն | hvala
благодаря | gràcies | hvala-děkuji | tak | dank-u | tänan | kiitos | merci
danke | ευχαριστώ | mahalo | תודה | धन्यवाद | köszönöm | takk
terima kasih | grazie | grazzi | ありがとうございました | paldies
감사합니다 | choukrane | ačiū | Баярлалаа | takk | хвала | dziękuję
obrigado | mulţumesc | спасибо | dakujem | hvala | gracias | tack | nandri
ขอบคุณ | teşekkür-ederim | Дякую | diolch | a dank | ngiyabonga | ধন্যবাদ
Дзякуй | ကျေးဇူးတင်ပါတယ် | salamat | děkuji | dankon | aitä | salamat
grazas | მადლობა | danke schön | આભાર | mèsi | na gode | ua tsaug
köszönöm | takk fyrir | daalu | goraibh maith agat | matur-nuwun
ধন্যবাদ | рахмет | spas | ຂອບໃຈ | gratias ago | tibi | благодарам
misaotra | നന്ദി | kia mihi | ممنون | zikomo | ممنون | ਧੰਨਵਾਦ ਹੋਵੇ | multumesc
спасибо теб | faafetai | tapadh-leat | хвала ти | ndatenda | مهربانی | ಧನ್ಯವಾದ
hvala timahadsanid | kea leboh hatur nuhun | asante | ташаккур | நன்றி
Дякую | شكريا | آپ کا | cảm on | diolch tankewol | enkosi | דאנקען
o şeun | | សូមអរគុណ | thank you